Personal Finance Essentials

Rick Scott

This book is designed to provide competent and general financial advice to US citizens. Readers should realize that the author is not a registered or certified financial advisor. The author does have a masters and doctoral degree in finance and has taught collegiate-level finance for over ten years.

Laws vary over time and from state to state. Individual financial situations are not the same. Therefore, if specific financial or legal advice is required, professional advisors should be employed. The author specifically disclaims any liability incurred from the use of this book.

Table of Contents

Foreword

In the eighties, I was in West Germany serving in the U.S. Army and making less than $10,000 a year. My room and board were paid for, and my expenses were low. I did have *not* inconsiderable nightlife expenses, but that was about it. I was saving for college, and I had some money that I wanted to invest. Unfortunately, I had only received two types of financial guidance in my youth: wrong and none.

I decided I needed a financial education. I started by acquiring information from reputable financial firms, but it turns out that gathering information from advertisements is not a great way to learn about personal finance. I decided to find a good book about personal finance. This task was more difficult at the time because there was no Amazon or online book reviews. Fortunately, I was able to find an excellent financial guide for the totally ignorant.

That book incentivized me to read a few more books about personal finance and investments. As a result, I started investing wisely and often. Eventually, I earned a Ph.D. in Finance, and now I delight in passing on my knowledge of personal finance to others.

Recently, I visited an old friend that was my roommate when I read that first personal finance book in Germany decades ago. During our roommate years, he was in the same boat as me. We were both college dropouts struggling in the Army with little to no financial knowledge. Now, he is a hugely successful entrepreneur that has sold one business for millions and started another company just for fun (although I am sure it will be profitable).

As we were riding to take a look at his new business, I mentioned that I was almost through with my personal finance book. He congratulated me and then thanked me for lending him that personal finance guide that I had read when we were roommates. I had forgotten about that. He said that the book had changed his life for the better as well. I do not doubt that he would have found his way to success anyway, but it felt good to realize that I may have helped him a bit by merely recommending a book.

I hope that this book will do for you what that book did for my friend and me. I hope that you learn that financial success does not happen by accident or without effort. Also, I want you to learn that you are in control of your future financial success and that you can succeed. This success requires knowledge and planning. If you read this book, you should know how to create a plan that will enable you to not be poor and get rich slowly.

This book is relatively short so that readers will be encouraged to read it, learn important concepts about personal finance, get rich slowly, and celebrate me as a hero. In this scenario, I end up as the Rose Bowl Grand Marshall at the end. I'm not sure what the Grand Marshall does, but rest assured, I will be ready when the time comes.

The last chapter in this book is a summary chapter. I advise you to read the whole book. If you got this book as a gift and you really don't feel like reading it, you can just read the last chapter and the short appendix. You should learn a lot of things that can help you and enable you to convince the gift giver that you have read the book. Hopefully, after reading the last chapter, you will want to read the rest of the book anyway. Enjoy!

Chapter 1: You Control Your Financial Destiny

Any Financial Plan is (Almost Always) Better than None

Building wealth is easy and fun.

Umm.

Mmm.

Actually, it is not. I read somewhere that you had to hook readers with the first sentence of your book, and I wanted you to start reading. If you have gotten this far, mission accomplished. I apologize for the prevarication, and I promise not to do it again, but well…mission accomplished.

The truth is that building wealth takes time, planning, and effort. That's the bad news. The good news is that building wealth is doable for almost everyone lucky enough to be residing in the U.S.A or other similarly free, primarily capitalist society. More good news is that this book is intended to teach you how to build wealth, and the methods are not that complicated.

This book is purposefully short. Once again, I want people to read this book, and I know that reading a book on personal finance is like eating broccoli to most people. You know it is good for you, but you don't really want to do it, and you are more likely to do it if there is a smaller amount.

If you are doing well or even great financially, you can still get something out of this book (besides a heart-warming sense of superiority). After all, if you learn something that improves your financial position by thousands of dollars, that will be worth your time and the cost of the book. If you don't learn anything from this book, then you have confirmed that you are very well-informed. Therefore, you can pass this book on to your friends and relatives that always seem to be having financial troubles.

This book can be small because it is *not* designed to tell you everything you ever need to know about personal finances. I follow the 80/20 rule. You should learn over 80% of what you need to know from this book while putting in less than 20% of the effort that you would reading a very comprehensive personal finance book. I also made it my goal to make this book as easy to read as possible while avoiding most of the grimy, boring, incomprehensible minutia that inhabits the financial world.

Accomplished personal trainers will tell you that the best workout regimen for their clients is the one their clients will follow. If they design a personal workout schedule that would be superb for professional athletes, it will probably be terrible for an average person. A typical person won't have the time or energy to follow the regimen, and they will end up quitting. Similarly, my goal is to provide a book that you will read and use. Hopefully, you will re-read it and give it as a gift to friends and relatives.

My goal is to get you hooked on making a purposeful financial plan for your future. If I succeed, you can read more in-depth books later if you want (and I hope you do). You never know, I might write one. If I don't, there are a myriad of excellent, in-depth personal finance books by the likes of Suze Orman, Dave Ramsey, and others.

There are diminishing returns to every finance book you read. If you read ten personal finance books, you will not know ten times as much about personal finance than if you had only read one good book. In fact, if you read a personal finance book that contains bad advice (and there are lots of them out there), you may end up making poorer financial decisions because of the bad information you garner. More importantly, there are numerous advertisements, blogs, and salespersons that offer lousy advice. You need to learn to ascertain the difference between good and bad advice.

I hope my book is your first step to developing your financial knowledge, but if it is your only step, you are ahead of most people. In fact, most people spend more time and effort shopping for holiday or birthday gifts than they do planning their finances. That's fine for the recipients, presumably someone you like, but if you take the time to plan your finances, you can afford better gifts (or keep the money yourself).

Making a financial plan is better than not making one. That seems obvious, right? Most of us have heard the adage "failing to plan is planning to fail." That is not only an adage but also a truism. Still, a large percentage of people (I would guess a majority) do not have a financial plan. That is unless you count the plan for what they are going to do with their money until their next paycheck. For the record, I do not count living paycheck to paycheck as financial planning.

If you have a financial plan and you are making a significant effort to follow it, you put yourself in a much better position than someone that has no plan or has a *laissez-faire* attitude about their personal finances. I'm not sure what the official definition of *laissez-faire* is (okay, okay, I guess I could have looked up the definition, but that would have ruined the joke that follows), but in this case, I define it as lazy and ignorant.

Many people fear making a financial plan because they think it will require them putting forth the effort to become a financial expert. That is simply not true. I have had many wonderful vacations over the years, but I am not a travel expert. I simply educated myself somewhat about the places I wanted to go, did a reasonable amount of research, asked others for recommendations, and enjoyed. Making and implementing a successful financial plan is not that different from planning and enjoying a vacation. If you put forth a reasonable amount of effort, you do not have to be an expert. If done correctly, the rewards greatly outweigh the effort.

If you are poor, does that mean you are unintelligent or lazy? Absolutely not. There are legions of intelligent poor people. There is also a multitude of hard-working poor people. There is also a copious amount of bright and diligent poor people. I like to think I used to be one. The primary reason that smart, industrious people remain poor is that they don't have an adequate education in personal finance.

So, why do so many people know so little about the vital topic of personal finance? Unfortunately, personal finance is rarely taught at the high school level or in lower grades. On the rare occasions when it is taught, it is often taught incorrectly. This means that the clear majority of students that don't go on to college have little or no education in personal finance. This group of people is likely to have a lower lifetime income and needs a personal financial education as much as anyone. There are sporadic efforts to include more personal financial education in public schools, but progress thus far has been minimal.

Personal finance is also rarely taught at the collegiate level. I have taught at two fine universities. At one university, a large state school, I taught an elective personal finance class that was held once a year. I thought that surely this class would be popular because it is such an important class that could improve the lives of the students. The reality is that way less than 1% (probably less than 0.1%) of the students at the university took the class before graduating. The reason was simple. It was not viewed as an easy "A," and the average student didn't understand the importance of proper personal financial planning.

At the other university where I have taught, a smaller private school, a personal finance class is not offered. The reason for this is simple. It is believed that students have little interest in enrolling in the class. I have given free seminars at the university, which support the idea that most students are indifferent to personal financial education. Therefore, I do my best to teach personal finance in my other finance classes. This works, but unfortunately, efforts at personal financial education only reach a relatively small number of business school students.

The lack of personal finance education opportunities and interest at the K-12 and collegiate educational levels partially explains how so many high-income individuals such as doctors and lawyers end up with financial difficulties or even bankruptcy. If high-earning individuals can make poor financial decisions that overwhelm their high income, what are the odds that middle-class or low-income individuals can build wealth? The answer is that it probably won't happen unless they educate themselves on personal finance issues. Pat yourself on the back now because you are currently in the process of educating yourself, but please keep reading because we are just getting started.

You are Responsible for Your Own Financial Freedom

If we aren't learning about financial planning in school, then where do we learn it? Often, we don't actively learn anything about personal finance. Yikes! Most of us learn about money management from our parents. That is fine if your parents are astute financial managers that make it a point to educate their children on all matters financial, but not so great for most of us. After all, if your parents aren't financially successful and not good at managing money, what can they teach their children (that is, if they are making an effort to teach their children about personal financial planning)?

So, let's suppose you were not taught how to manage your finances or were taught bad financial habits. If you are poor, is it your fault? Nope. If you stay poor, is it your fault? Probably. This may seem harsh, but some motivation can be garnered from this blame game.

Stay with me here because there will be a happy ending. Being poor is not a choice, but it is usually a result of a series of bad decisions. If you are poor, you or your parents have made poor financial decisions (barring major medical and other similar catastrophes).

I spent most of my teenage years living in poor neighborhoods. Frankly, almost everyone in my community complained about the government and wealthy people. I often heard and believed that the government should solve our problems. In retrospect, that benefitted none of us. Some of my friends and I decided to get an education or a technical skill that would afford us a reasonably good income. We also made reasonably good financial decisions. After a few years, the poor people from my old neighborhood that made good decisions slowly improved their financial lot. The ones that continued to complain, make poor financial decisions, and didn't try to improve their lives made no progress. They are still complaining that the rich people and the government should do more to make their lives better.

Personal responsibility is an essential key to success, financial or otherwise. If you don't blame others for your woes, you control your destiny. Not having money is temporary. Poor is a mindset that leads to permanence.

Here comes the happy ending part of achieving the goal of financial success. If other people are responsible for your lack of financial success, there is nothing you can do to change your circumstances. This is rarely the case. If you understand and believe that you are responsible for your financial success, there is nothing that can stop you from achieving financial security. That is called empowerment, and it is a beautiful thing.

If you put yourself in a position to make a reasonably good living, save your money, and invest wisely, you will put yourself on the road to financial success. I have done it, and I have met hundreds of others that have done it. The first step to financial success is believing you have control of your future. If you think that your decisions have a significant impact on your financial success, you are correct, and you are on your way to being financially secure. Anyone can work for money; smart people learn how to make money work for them.

This book is designed to teach how to prevent habits that perpetuate poverty and learn habits that increase wealth. The methods I teach do not lead to instant wealth. My goal is to teach people how to stop being poor and get rich *slowly*.

What? Slowly? Who wants that? You probably do.

There are ways for the average person to get rich quickly, but they almost always involve significant risk. If you have an unusual athletic or artistic talent, sometimes you can take the highway to riches. If you come up with a great invention or concept that gives you an edge over all your business competition, you could be flashing your exorbitant bling at the cotillion in no time.

Other methods of getting rich involve great expertise in a given field, borrowed money, and the risk of losing everything. If that's in your DNA, go for it. There are plenty of successful people that risk bankruptcy and succeed. Many successful people don't mind sharing that they went bankrupt several times on their way to success. Good for them.

That is not my way, nor is it the way that most of us want to proceed through life. I have derived a great deal of satisfaction from my life consistently getting better financially through the years. After being poor for most of my first quarter-century on this earth, I don't think I would have dealt well with being broke at age 40 after my third business went bankrupt.

Getting rich *slowly* is still getting rich, and if you are enjoying yourself along the way, it is a great way to go. I highly recommend it. I took the slow road to wealth. I didn't start down this road until I realized that I controlled my financial destiny. The first step was to acquire an education that would lead to a better job.

My education has paid off personally and professionally. I was flat broke upon acquiring my undergraduate degree at age 26. Actually, I was not flat broke because I had an $800 car (on a good day) and a $190 wardrobe (this estimate is generous), but I had $1,000 in credit card debt and a few thousand dollars in student debt. I was worth less than nothing. Things got better, but not immediately.

Soon, I was even more in debt, although I was finally driving a car worth more than a grand. It was a 2-year-old Toyota Corolla four-door. The *chicks* were not as impressed as I thought they would be. Of course, I no longer call women *chicks*, but they still have never been particularly impressed by me or my car, not even my hail-damaged Volkswagen convertible that I was driving when I met my beautiful wife.

Still, things did turn around. I finally had an education, even if I had been on the 8-year plan because I took time out to make college money in the military. A quality education is almost always a good investment. My education began to pay off almost immediately as my salary tripled within a few years. A little over a year after my graduation, I started to save money. What a concept!

I had a positive net worth, which means I had more money saved than I had debt. Hallelujah, praise Jesus (or your preferred Messiah, Deity, or lack thereof)! The train was a-rollin'. My extensive readings had taught me that if you earned more than you spent and you invested the difference wisely, you slowly (sometimes, oh so slowly) got rich.

I want to interrupt this *enthralling* recollection of my life events to emphasize some crucial points that are surprisingly difficult to grasp. If you earn more than you spend and invest the difference wisely, you get rich. If you earn a lot more than you spend, you tend to get rich very quickly. If you invest very wisely, you tend to get rich more quickly. It is valuable to note that it is much easier to spend wisely (and thus save more) than to invest wisely or earn more money. Saving and investing are good ideas. The primary purpose of this book is to teach you how to do both well.

Let's get back to my developing life story. I earned more and more from year to year. Most people do this. I saved more and more from year to year. Most people do not do this, go figure. Because I earned more and saved more, I managed to amass a sizable, though not exorbitant, net worth. My wealth was greatly enhanced by following the advice I had garnered from extensive readings about the investment industry. This occurred despite my costly proclivity for moving regularly (I was a wanderer) and an even more expensive divorce.

Money provides freedom. When I was a kid, having money meant I had the freedom to purchase an ice cream or another treat. I used ice cream cones as a tool to understand prices. Back then, an ice cream cone cost $0.25. If I found a toy that cost $2.00 that I wanted, I had a decision to make. Would I rather have the toy or eight ice cream cones? This seems weird. Okay, it was and is weird, but it helped me to learn the value of money and how to make sound financial choices. For example, I have always wanted a Lamborghini, but when I have compared the costs of a supercar to all my other wants, I continue to drive my practical automobile. Hey, it is dependable and has a great sound system.

As an adult, money can provide many, more important freedoms. It can provide the freedom to change careers, get an education, retire when you want, and to help others. It also can offer the freedom to take vacations, spend more time with family, and pursue hobbies.

Personally, I earned and saved enough money in my twenties and thirties to be able to afford to pursue my dreams in my forties. Within ten years starting at age 39, I got married, had two kids, earned a Ph.D. in finance, and began a career as a college professor. There is no way I could have accomplished these goals without money (and lots of it). Money gave me freedom.

Even though money provides freedom, it is important to reemphasize that money does not equal happiness. It is easier to be happy if you do not have financial worries. Still, many people live a long, happy life without riches, and many rich people live miserable lives. Striving to succeed financially is a worthy goal, but it is foolish to put it above happiness and ethical, honorable behavior.

If You Don't Save Money, You Will Always Be Poor

An essential goal of anyone that is having financial difficulty should be to get out of debt and start saving money. If you don't save money, you will always be poor. That is a monumentally important statement to understand. For emphasis, I am going to give the statement its own paragraph bolded and in italics.

If you don't save money, you will always be poor.

Maybe I should have underlined the sentence. I can't overemphasize the importance of this point. A lack of understanding of this simple fact is why so many people remain poor.

If you spend all your income, no amount of income will be enough to make you rich. Many people say that they could save money if they only had a higher salary, but when they get a raise or their income increases in some other way, they spend more money. Many people say that they cannot save money because their income is too low.

Here is an example using hypothetical numbers. The numbers are not significant, but the concept they demonstrate is essential to escaping poverty. Let's say your take-home pay is $30,000 a year ($2,500 a month). That is not a massive income. Most people that make that much money do not save money. If you ask them why, they will tell you that they can't possibly spend less, and they only make enough income to make ends meet.

Now, ask these same people what would happen if their take-home pay was $28,000 a year ($2,333 a month). The usual answer is that they would find a way to survive. They would eat less expensive food, find a cheaper place to live, take public transportation, get a roommate or something. They would find a way to survive, and they wouldn't end up living in a homeless shelter.

Well, if they can make it on $28,000 a year, why can't they save money if they are making $30,000 a year. The answer is that they *can* save money while making $30,000 a year, but they would rather spend all their income on things that make life more enjoyable. That is understandable, but it ensures that the person will remain in poverty. Remember the key point I emphasized earlier: ***If you don't save money, you will always be poor.***

There are people out there making $200,000 a year, and they still have no savings. I don't know how they manage to do it, but it happens. These people are living a life of luxury, but in some sense, they are poor. Sometimes, people in this situation lose their job or another source of income, and they are soon bankrupt. Insane? Yes. They weren't saving money, and they were poor. They were simply unaware that they were poor until after the income dried up.

It is well-documented that many professional athletes, famous artists, and lottery winners end up bankrupt. A lack of money is not why these tragedies occur. It is a lack of saving and investing. They manage to spend more than they have no matter how much they have. They didn't save, and so they ended up destitute.

It has been estimated that two-thirds of households would not be able to cover an unexpected $1,000 expense. Medical expenses, car repairs, or home repairs can easily exceed this amount. Therefore, many people are not equipped to deal financially with reality. You do not want to be in this group.

Your first savings goal should be to have 3 to 6 months' worth of living expenses in emergency savings. It is okay to have up to a year's worth of emergency savings, but you shouldn't have more than that. The reason for this is that emergency savings have to be readily accessible. Therefore, emergency savings generally earn a lower rate of return than other investments.

Emergency savings are typically deposited in checking accounts, savings accounts, bank certificate of deposits (CDs), and money market funds. It is a good idea to create a separate account for emergency savings. Therefore, I do not recommend using a checking account.

When you get a raise or extra money from an unexpected source, save some and use some for fun. This will allow you to improve your life in two ways. You enjoy life more today, and you are saving so that you can enjoy your life more in the future. Future you will thank present-day you someday.

Don't try to keep up with the Joneses. If you decide to get a luxury car only because your friends or neighbors are doing so, that is not a good decision-making process. Your friends may or may not be able to afford luxurious living, but that doesn't matter. What matters is: "Can you afford it?" If you want to keep up with the Joneses, you may keep up with them into surefire poorness.

One more time: ***If you don't save money, you will always be poor.***

Saving money might seem like an impossible dream if you are already in debt, but debt is not a life sentence. Despite this, many people choose to make debt a life sentence by continually borrowing throughout their entire life even when they do not need to do so. These people need advice and guidance.

If you are already at a point where you cannot possibly pay off your debts, there is help available. Your credit will probably be impaired, but debt problems do not go away on their own accord. You need to act to take care of your debt problems. There are numerous consumer credit counseling services out there, many of them are very helpful, and some of them create further misery. If you need such assistance, you should make sure you are using a useful service.

The National Foundation for Consumer Credit (NFCC) (nfcc.org) can assist you in finding a good credit counseling organization. If a counseling agency is a Consumer Credit Counseling Service (CCCS) agency, then they are a member of the NFCC, and they are a non-profit.

Other non-profit organizations will aid in providing advice on how to deal with overwhelming debt problems. They include American Consumer Credit Counseling (consumercredit.com), InCharge Institute of America (incharge.org), and Money Management International (moneymanagement.org). Dave Ramsey, (daveramsey.com), offers excellent Christian-based methods to conquer debt problems. If you are not a Christian, no worries, his techniques will work for anyone.

Be very wary of any organization that offers to solve your debt problems for an up-front fee. There is an excellent chance that you will lose the money you paid and that your debt problems will not improve or will worsen.

Okay, here it is for the last time (actually probably not): ***If you don't save money, you will always be poor.***

Chapter 2: Financial and Lifestyle Decisions: They are Linked

Education and Career: Making Money is Important, and It Can Be Fun

Education is awesome. I earned a bachelor's degree in computer science in my twenties with four years in the military in the middle. Completing my first college degree is the primary reason I escaped poverty. Still, it is essential to know that a college education does not guarantee financial success.

I was poor when I was young. I decided as a teenager that I preferred not to be poor. Unfortunately, I didn't have a lot of guidance on how to not be poor. I read a lot, and I learned.

The first important thing that I learned was to invest in your education and find a career that you enjoy to a certain degree that will pay you a reasonable wage. That is not a particularly easy thing to do, but it is crucial. If you do not enjoy your career to a certain extent, you will be spending approximately one-third of your waking life doing something unpleasant. That is not a great long-term plan. On the other hand, if you love doing something that no one wants to pay you a living wage for, that is probably a worse plan.

The trade-off between enjoying your work and making more money is a tricky one with no answer that suits everyone. Therefore, it is worthwhile to spend a lot of effort and thought into considering your career course. Importantly, it is okay if you do not initially make the correct career choice. The important thing is that you either gain experience that will make you more valuable in your next job or make enough money to make the job worth it. You can always change your career choice.

Changing careers is becoming a typical course of action. It is preferable to enter your ideal career path earlier in your life, but it takes a little longer to find your way. Still, it is better to make progress. I spent the first half of my career as a computer systems analyst, and I have spent the last half of my career (so far) as a financial professional. Would I have been more successful if I had entered the finance profession in my twenties? The answer is almost certainly yes. Still, I am quite happy that I made the switch into my true passion when I did, rather than not at all.

You should evaluate your career path regularly, at least yearly. Of course, you shouldn't make a move on an impulse or because you had a bad month. Changing jobs or careers should be a decision that you spend several months or more considering. I spent several years considering my career change from computer systems analyst to finance, and that was a good idea. Once I made a move, I knew it was the right choice for me, and that confidence helped me to become successful in my new career.

I am a big believer in using education to improve your financial situation. I have made some mistakes in my educational journey, but I firmly believe that earning a quality education is the number one reason I have moved from being poor to being financially secure. If you are unsatisfied with your career and you think more training can improve your situation, you should strongly consider taking action. If you can create the opportunity to move towards a happier, more prosperous career, paying for your education will probably be the best investment you ever make.

If you want to start a new career, education is often a prerequisite. An investment in training for a career that you want to pursue is usually money well-spent. Education is often quite expensive in terms of time and money. Therefore, you should contemplate your options. For many educational programs, there are local or online options. You should shop around for your educational opportunities just like you would for any other consumer good.

Consider the value, convenience, and cost of the school you are considering attending. Don't fall into the trap that so many students do today of ignoring costs that you can borrow today. The government makes most college loans. The problem with this is that if you owe the government money, you must pay it back. Much like owing back taxes, outstanding student loans must be paid back sooner or later. Even bankruptcy usually does not make this debt go away.

Borrowing money to finance an a degree that will not meaningfully improve your employment prospects can lead to years of financial struggles. Future earnings prospects are greatly influenced by your choice of major, school choice, and grades (usually in that order). Also, people commonly list quitting school as one of their main regrets. That is exacerbated if you left school after you have run up sizable student loans. If you start school, start with a plan to complete school.

I have a bachelors, two masters, and a doctoral degree. I believe they all improved my earnings potential somewhat, but there was not a direct correlation between my educational achievement and my income. I primarily chose my undergraduate major in computer science because it was a major that usually led to a well-paying job at the time.

My choice was practical but somewhat short-sighted. I wanted to make money, but I did not want to spend the rest of my life as a systems analyst. My true passion was and is finance and investments. After earning graduate degrees that facilitated my switch into the finance field, I began to enjoy work a lot more. It is tough to put a price on increased enjoyment in the workplace, but it is a precious thing.

After I had successfully switched into a finance career, I proudly asked my wife, "Finance is less nerdy than computer science, don't you think?" She looked at me somewhat confused, shook her head slowly, and answered, "not really." Okay, not cooler, but I enjoyed work more.

Anything you can do to increase your income and/or increase your work satisfaction is worth doing. It doesn't happen on its own, though. It takes planning, and research and mistakes are often made. I have certainly taken jobs that turned out to be a step back, but usually, the career choices I have made have worked out. One important thing to know is that you should never settle for a job that makes you feel trapped or inadequate. You may have to suck it up for a while until you find a better alternative, but you should not accept a fate of low-paying, unsatisfying work. Life is too short to spend almost one-third of your life doing something unsatisfying.

Education is the most common way to increase income and job satisfaction, but it is certainly not the only way. Even if you are in your forties or fifties, it is not too late to earn another degree or otherwise educate yourself. I earned my undergraduate degree at age 26, my first master's degree at age 40, and my Ph.D. at 49. Sure, I wish I would have earned these degrees earlier, but I am pleased that I didn't wait later to obtain them. It is a beautiful thing not to dread going to work.

You should never stop considering options that might raise your income or career satisfaction.

Choosing a career is tough for most people. Man, is it tough? I have had a pretty successful career, but it could have been so much more successful if I had made better career choices. It is difficult to know what you want to do with the rest of your life when you begin. Many people end up working in careers that didn't exist when they were young.

I remember graduating high school without any tangible ideas about what I should do for a career. I had virtually no guidance from my elders, and it showed. Here are my undergraduate majors in chronological order: psychology, computer science, business management, undecided (finally, some honesty), accounting, electronics repair, computer science. I attended three undergraduate schools full-time for at least one semester. I attended a few other universities part-time. I finally earned my undergraduate degree in computer science.

Clearly, I didn't know what I wanted to do. My primary goal was to start making some serious coin. I finally chose computer science because, in the mid-eighties, this was considered a major that would allow you the opportunity to get a reasonably well-paying job. At the time, that was pretty much my only goal, to be reasonably paid. Yeah, I was not planning for the extended future.

Despite all my missteps, my career did get started on a stable path. One of the reasons that I was eventually successful was that I didn't lose sight of the most critical goal of attending college, *graduating*. Let me do that emphasis thing again.

If you decide to attend college, the most crucial goal is to graduate. If you don't graduate, you may end up having to pay back student loans without increasing your earnings potential. That is called going backward.

It is important to note that not everyone benefits from enrolling at a four-year collegiate program. There are many technical school and apprenticeship programs that will help a person more than a four-year program if they are so inclined. Many careers that do not require bachelors degrees, such as plumbing, electrical work, and automotive repair, can be financially, intellectually, and emotionally rewarding.

On the other hand, there are certainly a lot of four-year undergraduate degrees that do little to prepare their students for practical work. I could name some majors, but I work in the education industry, and I prefer not to be burned in effigy by my colleagues. If you do just a little research, you can probably find some undergraduate majors that do little to increase the income of their graduates.

No matter what your major or program, it is better to graduate from some program once you start. It demonstrates to employers that you can finish something once you get started. Employers like that.

Many people cite examples of people that dropped out of school and yet were still fabulously successful (Bill Gates, Michael Dell, Richard Branson) to rationalize quitting. For every one of these successes, I can cite a million dropouts that had fabulously unsuccessful careers. It might take me a while, but I can do it.

So, if you are a hard-working, passionate, genius with a revolutionary business idea, you should consider dropping out of school. Otherwise, finish the drill.

Choosing a career is problematic for most people because most people do not have an overwhelming passion for a career. If you have a passion for a career that offers you reasonable employment stability, income, and job satisfaction, you are way ahead of the game. Congratulations!

I recently talked to a high school senior, Emma, that realized from an early age that she wanted to be a veterinarian. This job is and will be in demand. It also offers substantial income opportunities. Furthermore, it provides a pleasant working environment with reasonable hours and regular vacations. Jackpot!

When considering a career, you should consider all facets of that career: income, employment stability, location, hours, work environment, etc. There is a lot to balance there.

Emma had a passion for a career that offered great rewards, but that wasn't enough. Emma also was an excellent student that volunteered at animal shelters. She earned acceptance at a top veterinary program, and she was well on her way to a successful career. Many teens want to be a veterinarian, but few have the intelligence and drive to make it happen.

It would be wonderful if all of us had a passion from an early age for a realistic, lucrative career, which would provide us with tremendous job satisfaction. Sadly, this is not true for most of us. If it is true for you, then consider yourself blessed and keep on trucking. It is terrific if you have a passion for a career that will reward you financially, personally, and psychologically, but most of us must strike a balance between career goals.

Striking a balance among career goals and passions is usually quite tricky. Still, we must strive to figure it out. Until we figure it out, we must make a living, and that should be our initial concern. It took me decades to figure it out, but I am glad I finally did. If you do not have 100% job satisfaction, you should continue to strive to improve your career. You should continually look for improved career opportunities. Still, I'd advise you never to quit a job until you have a new one (unless there are extraordinary circumstances).

You should know the difference between a job and a career. A job is something you do to earn enough money to survive or move ahead in life. A job does not necessarily have to be unenjoyable.

When I was in college in my early twenties, I had a job at a convenience store on the overnight shift. It turned out to be an enjoyable job. The pace was slow, so I had time to read, and I read newspapers and business publications that the store sold. I loved that. Have I mentioned that I am a nerd? I also ended up dating several attractive customers that I met on the job. *L'amour* is for the young. Okay, I'm wasn't a super-nerd. Still, this job was just something I was doing until I could do what I really wanted to do, start a career.

A career is a job or succession of jobs that moves you towards your dream job (the culmination of a career). A career usually requires specialized training and a sequence of promotions or job changes in which you, hopefully, make progress towards your goal. Most desirable careers require advanced education or an apprenticeship, along with years of learning the ropes of that profession.

My job at the convenience store helped my career because it provided money for me to complete my education, but it was just a job. It did not significantly move me towards my career goal in my first career as a systems analyst or my second career as a financial professional, but it was still a good job. Sometimes, if a job allows you to earn money when you need it, that's a good job.

As much as I appreciated my job at the convenience store, an event occurred that made me realize it was just a job. In the smallish city where I attended college, there were only three convenience stores that were open all night. In one of those stores, the clerk was shot in a robbery early in the morning on a night I was working. I did the math. I had a one out of three chance of being shot that night, but I was lucky. Soon, I put in my two-weeks' notice. After all, it was just a job, and I could read at the library.

If you have a job to help you get an education or overcome an obstacle or financial difficulties, that is okay. If you have a job and you have settled into a lifestyle where that job is not propelling you towards a higher goal, that is called a rut, and it is not okay. Once you have your education, take employment that will improve your career and move you towards your ultimate goals.

If you are thinking about attending college, it is excellent if you are passionate about a major that is likely to prepare you for a lucrative career. You have hit the lottery. If you don't have any particular passion for a career, at least not one likely to offer a reasonable income, that's too bad. But you are in the same boat as the rest of us.

I did a lot of research into my undergraduate major. Yet, I still did not choose a major that was optimal for me. I chose well enough to start a career that provided enough income until I figured out what career was right for me. I also saved enough to make that new career happen. My mistakes offer an example that even if you do not choose the perfect educational path, it should be okay if you do a reasonably good job.

When choosing a career path, avoid selecting a career that pays well but makes you miserable. Similarly, you should avoid choosing something that is fun but doesn't pay you enough to reach your financial goals. For most of us, this is not an easy thing to do. Therefore, you need to do your homework.

Make a list of jobs that might interest you by going through a list of positions or majors on the internet or from other sources. After finding a field you are interested in, find out information about the career such as education requirements, typically pay, potential positions it can lead to, and the overall outlook of the field. For example, truck driving might be a satisfying career for some over the next ten years. But self-driving trucks are coming, so it is unlikely to be an excellent long-term career.

Talk to several people that have that career. Ask questions. Most people are happy to give you a little career advice. If you get it wrong, you can probably recover, especially if you are young. The worst thing you can do is remain in a job that makes you miserable, either because it is unsatisfying, or the pay is too meager.

If you decide to pursue higher education, do everything you can to keep your student debt and debt in general low. Currently, most student debt cannot be erased in bankruptcy. It is like owing the government back taxes. It is tough to make it go away even if you can't pay it. Many people have ruined their lives by incurring massive debt to get an education that did not lead to a job with sufficient pay. Don't be one of them.

Once you have decided on a career and prepared to start, you will likely have some decisions to make. If you are looking for a job, work hard at finding one. Don't quit your current job until you find a new one. I didn't follow this advice twice in my career, leaving my old job before I had a new one. Things ended well for me both times, but there was tremendous anxiety as the bills kept coming in while the income to pay them did not.

If you are unemployed, you should treat looking for employment as your employment. That means you should spend 40 hours or more per week searching for a job and researching the best ways to find one. Only making up a standard resume and cover letter and putting it out on the web will not do.

You should scour the web and other sources looking for opportunities. You should tell all your friends, relatives, and acquaintances that you are looking for work and what type of work you are seeking. I got the best systems analyst job I ever had because I mentioned that I was looking for work to a small group of acquaintances.

Once you find opportunities, create a customized application, resume, and cover letter for that job. Research current job-seeking tips. Don't pay an employment company (placement office) upfront money to find you a job. Work-at-home offers are often a scam, but at-home customer service jobs are on the rise.

When interviewing for a position, do your best to get the offer. If you act like you are not sure if you are interested in the job, it will likely be offered to someone that is interested. After you get the offer, then decide if you want the job or not and be honest in your negotiations.

When considering a job, the compensation level is significant, but it is not everything. Consider all aspects of the situation: location, hours, work environment, stability, advancement opportunities, and more. Employment benefits are important. Always consider them when choosing a job.

If you want to take an unconventional path such as traveling or starting a business, it is often best to do that early before you have financial and family responsibilities. If you start a business right after college, and it fails after a couple of years, many employers will be impressed by your initiative and ambition. Of course, if it doesn't fail, that is even better. If you take three months to travel in Europe after college, most potential employers will understand (and probably be a little envious).

Starting your own business is a way to avoid taxes, get rich quickly and fabulously, or go broke quickly (or slowly and painfully). Owning your own business is a faster way to riches, but it is riskier, and you must know the risks. When other job prospects are slim, many think it is a good idea to start a business. That may be true, but most new businesses fail within a few years. If you choose to start a business, you must be prepared to lose your entire investment. Hopefully, that won't happen, but it is a real possibility. Proceed with caution.

Only start a new business if you have done your homework and are prepared to work long hours (your competitors will be doing so). Starting your own business is a topic for other books or years of education.

Once you get going in a career, you will still likely have decisions to make. Even if you enjoy your job, you should still assess regularly (at least once a year) if there are better options out there. Also, even if you decide that you are happy with your job, you should assess the future of your position.

In the nineties, I was working for a firm that was trying to reduce its systems analyst headcount through various methods. I did my homework and accepted a buyout that gave me nine month's pay. Cha-ching! I then found a job with an information technology outsourcing firm at increased pay. Within a year, the members of my old workgroup were all outsourced. They did not receive any extra payment. A little over a year later, I was back working for my original firm as a contractor at increased pay with better benefits.

The point is not that I am a genius that made an exquisitely excellent career decision. My wonderful wife and two delightful children would likely dispute the genius part. The point is that it is essential to stay informed about your company, career, and the economy in general. Ignorance is rarely blissful in the long-run.

Changing jobs is fine but do it with a purpose such as improved salary or increased job satisfaction. Don't job hop. After you start your career, expect to be asked about anytime that you work for a company for less than two years. There are correct answers for why you move on from a company: better pay, better lifestyle, more responsibility, better fit, and many more. Still, most employers want to see a certain amount of stability in their potential employee's career path.

Passion in a career is important. Life is so much easier if you do not dread going to work each day. I tell my students that I enjoy my job, but that if I weren't getting paid to be in class, I'd be at the beach. It's true. Still, this means that I have a good job. I have had employment in the past, where I dreaded going to work each day and counted the hours until I could leave work. That is no way to live.

It is vital to avoid putting yourself in a position where you must keep working at a job you hate. I have known dozens of people that continue working at a job that they dreaded for decades. Frequently, they complained that their work was worth so much more than they were getting paid. In a free-market economy, people are generally paid what they are worth. Therefore, if you think you are woefully underpaid, you should consider other options.

If you avoid excessive debt and other financial obligations, it will help to avoid becoming trapped in a job that you dread. If you achieve that, it is no small feat.

So, let's say things are going well, but you are not completely happy. Your job is fine. You are making decent coin. You saved up and invested a significant amount. Still, you have some career dreams that are not being fulfilled.

Well, if you have saved enough money and you want to make a move, make it. Of course, you want to analyze any significant changes in detail.

After earning my undergraduate degree in my twenties, I believed that I wanted to be a college professor. I took graduate tests and explored graduate schools. Then I got a job and got addicted to the mediocre money. Being not poor is a great thing.

Still, the idea of being a college professor never went away. It was my dream. Eventually, I realized that I had a much greater passion for finance than I did for computer systems analysis. In my early forties, I realized that I wanted to be a finance professor, and I was going to make it happen.

I had saved a large amount of money through the years and invested it wisely. Therefore, I believed I had enough money to make my dream happen. I applied to a doctoral program in finance, and I was accepted. I decided to quit my job and go back to school full-time for a program that would last at least four years.

I told my wife my plans. She was not particularly enthusiastic, but she was supportive. We had two young children, so that made sense. My wife's parents and my Dad had similar responses. "Are you sure?" "Have you thought this through?"

Their concern was well-intentioned and understandable. But they did not know that I had planned and invested for years. They didn't know that I had done my homework on the odds of success of my career switch. Also, they did not understand my desire to escape a career that had become untenable. They came from a generation where you would never leave a job that provided financial security. I wanted more than financial security. What an improvement over merely wishing not to be poor.

My career switch is instructive. If you save your money and invest it wisely, keep your debts and financial obligations low, and do your research and plan well, you will better be able to make your dream job happen.

If you put yourself in a position where you have the financial wherewithal to follow your dream, you can make it happen. For most of us, it is not a short or easy road, but it is a road worth building and taking.

Important Personal and Financial Decisions: Marriage, Kids, Friends, and Relatives

Most people make the two most important financial decisions of their life with little or no regard to the financial implications. That's not wise.

The most important financial decision a person makes is usually their choice of a mate. That's right, the person you marry or otherwise hook up with for several years has a massive effect on your financial welfare. That's kind of a "no, duh" when you think about it.

So, why do so many people not think about it? Well, because most of us do not think about our choice of a mate as mainly a financial decision. As well, we shouldn't. The choice of a mate should *not* be *primarily* a financial decision. It should mostly be based on other factors such as love, character, honesty, dependability, and compatibility. Still, deciding on a mate without considering the financial implications is unwise. Thanks, Mr. Romance Killer.

I am old enough (so old!) to have seen how these things often go. A financially stable person marries someone that doesn't seem to be able to hold a job, has little ambition, spends too much, has excessive debt, doesn't manage money well, and is otherwise a financial disaster. The stable person thinks they will be able to change the other person because they love each other, and the person really, really wants to change to prove their love. Yeah, good luck with that. Most people don't want to alter their core character. If they did, they would have done it already.

In my twenties, I became friends with a couple of married co-workers in their late thirties that were very much in love. They were both making very substantial salaries. I noticed that my male friend had traded in his beloved sports car for a practical vehicle. He confided in me that his wife had a spending problem and had ran up substantial credit card debt that caused them to cut back. He stated that she had a credit card problem when they married, but he thought she had it under control. He felt that they were going to be okay now that they had discussed the issue, and she had promised not to buy anything that was not in their budget.

Less than a year later, they got divorced. My friend said his wife had rented a P.O. box so that she could apply for new credit cards without his knowledge, and she spent them all to the limit. He didn't find out until he started getting collection notices. They declared bankruptcy and got divorced. It was devastating to my friend emotionally and financially.

He had chosen to ignore a severe psychological spending problem his wife had in the hopes it would get better. It got worse.

Ignoring financial problems that a potential spouse has is not that different than ignoring substance abuse problems that a prospective spouse has. Ignoring either is quite unwise.

It is a good rule of thumb to realize that whatever problems a potential mate has, financial or otherwise, they do not tend to go away once you marry that person. If anything, they usually tend to worsen.

Now, I want to emphasize that a good relationship need not go bad over financial problems, especially minor ones. Relationship and financial counseling are available and should be used when the relationship is worth saving. There is no ignoring the fact that financial problems are one of the most common, probably the most common reason for relationship problems.

The second most important financial decision most people make is whether to have or adopt children. Of course, this is not a purely financial decision. My beautiful bride and I have two teenage children. We realized when we planned our little family that these kids would cost us some money. Boy, have they? They have been cash-flow negative from the word "go." We anticipate no positive-cash flow years from them in the foreseeable future.

Still, they are easily the best investment we have ever made. There is no price for the joy they have brought us. As an additional bonus, we are hoping that we can guilt them into assisting us in our dotage if we need their help. Cha-Ching!

Having children is costly. Almost all of them generate negative cash flows for twenty-plus years. They do have their good points. You get a nice little tax break when you have children. Also, that unconditional love thing is pretty sweet.

Every few years, a big news story comes out that says something along the lines of "it cost $1.2 million to raise a child until they graduate college. When I hear these outlandish stories, I know it is an example of a reporter creating hyperbolic news from a bad scientific study (a common practice for many news outlets). Believe me, if it cost that much to raise a child, there would be a lot fewer children. It is ridiculous on its face. Now, if you choose to, you can spend a million dollars raising a child. It wouldn't even be that hard if you send them to ultra-expensive private schools and colleges. Still, children can be raised well on a lot less money. Sometimes, they save you money by preventing you from going out to expensive dinners and spending money on exotic vacations and luxury sports cars (sigh). Don't let the hyperbolic news stories prevent you from having children if you so desire.

Of course, having children is *not* primarily a financial decision. If it were, no one in their right mind would ever have children. Still, it is wise to avoid having children until you can afford to take care of them.

My wife and I did not have children until we were both in our late thirties. This was not any part of a grand plan. We didn't meet until we were well into our thirties. By the time we had kids, we were well able to afford children. Having children is challenging. It is much easier to face these challenges if you do not have significant financial stresses to add to the challenges.

If you already have children and you are struggling financially, there is an added need for you to manage your finances well. If this is you, you have my congratulations on taking steps to learn how to manage your money more effectively.

Yes, children are a constant expense, but if you do it right, it is money well spent. I consider working with my wife to raise our two teenage children to be the most important thing I have ever done (even though we are not done raising them yet). They have brought me countless moments of joy, and the joyful moments continue daily. You can't put a price on these things, but I know the value of my children to me and my wife dramatically exceeds all the expenses. Also, you never know, you might appreciate having them when you are old, and you need a little help.

If you have kids, you should teach them about managing money. There are numerous web resources and books that explain how to help your kids learn about finances. Some are better than others, but you will almost certainly prepare your children better for life if you do something rather than doing little or nothing.

One of my favorite resources is a free website, Warren Buffett's Secret Millionaires Club ® (smckids.com). Warren Buffett is one of the most successful investors of all time and the ultra-successful chief executive officer (CEO) of Berkshire Hathaway (subsidiaries include GEICO, Burlington Northern Santa Fe Railroad, Dairy Queen, and dozens of other major companies). The website consists of 26 short videos (more may be added later) that teach "the basics of good financial decision making and some of the basic lessons of starting a business."

Dave Ramsey also sells numerous resources for educating children about finance (daveramsey.com/store/kids-teens/cYouth.html). Ramsey offers consistently reliable and valuable advice about personal financial management.

I have found that an excellent way to educate my children about finances is to discuss family financial matters with them. Of course, I do not provide details, and the discussions are quite general. I don't advise discussing your family's finances in detail if you are under financial stress. Navigating childhood is tough enough without having to worry about financial matters that you cannot control.

I enjoy telling my children about stock investments I have made for our family's benefit. It leads to interesting conversations as my children ask me how investments work and how do we use the money from the investments. For example, I tell my children we own stock in Disney. Then I am flooded with questions. What does it mean to own stock in Disney? What are the benefits? What are dividends? If some stocks don't pay dividends, what is the advantage of owning them? My children are mere teenagers, and they already understand investments better than the average adult. I plan for them to be fully capable of managing their finances by the time that they graduate from college. If they cannot do this, I haven't done my job. One thing I plan to require from them is that they read this book and give me feedback. Hi Kids!

The most important decision that most people make, the choice of a mate, and the second most important decision that most people make, the decision to have children are highly related. If you make a poor choice on your mate (or lack thereof), providing for any children you choose to have becomes much more difficult.

Frequently, the financial problems for children of unmarried parents pale in comparison to the personal and psychological difficulties they often face. Personally, my childhood was marred by the all too common American phenomena of a divorce resulting in poverty and parents that were constantly bickering with the children in the middle. Yuck!

This is a book on personal finance, but I would be derelict if I didn't address these essential personal issues that have a tremendous impact on finances and happiness. After all, the goal of financial success should be happiness.

If you choose to marry, choose your spouse wisely. If you have psychological problems, address those before you get married (yes, this probably means therapy and research of some type). If you want to have children, make sure you have them for the right reasons (more research and therapy).

Here are some critical points to consider when assessing the impact of marital and parental decisions on your financial health. Single parenthood is the most common cause of poverty. There is no way to sugarcoat this. It is much easier to raise kids if there are two parents.

Divorce is almost always terrible. It is difficult for the divorcing spouses and usually worse for the kids. You should put a significant amount of effort into avoiding divorce. If you do have to get divorced and you have children, do all you can to make it easy for the kids. They are innocent. You may have to make some significant sacrifices for your kids. *You should do it*. I love money, but no amount of money is more important than your children knowing that you love them.

If you are getting divorced, make immediate moves to protect yourself financially. Close joint accounts. Consult an attorney.

I am pleased to be nearing the end of this section because I have had to address painful personal issues that are intertwined with finances.

Marriage and children can be looked at in two ways. I think of my marriage and my children as the best things I have ever done. Even though I take a certain joy in reminding my kids that they are cash-flow negative, they don't seem to mind.

On the other hand, marriages can end in divorce, and children can become an economic argument between parents. The bottom line is that separating personal and financial decisions is not possible. This book does not directly address making sound personal decisions. My wife is a psychologist, and she would have better advice in this field. Still, I strongly encourage you to make wise personal decisions, especially when considering a spouse or children. If you do so, sound financial choices become much more likely.

Comedian Adam (Ace) Carolla has said, "if it doesn't make you happy or make you money, don't do it." I think he makes a good point. It is important to note that he is not just talking about the here and now.

The act of doing push-ups doesn't make the average person happy. Oh, if only it did. Still, the results from the push-ups often can make you happy in the future because you will have an improved appearance and added strength and energy. Similarly, most of us don't relish paying for and going to college, except for the occasional related party. But the results of our education should lead to greater happiness and more money.

Carolla is talking about getting caught up in doing things that don't benefit you in the short-term or long-term. For example, giving the finger to someone that cuts you off is unlikely to help you in any way and can lead to you becoming a victim of road-rage. Once, in my younger days, I honked repeatedly at someone that I thought had made a driving error. The next day, one of my best work friends told me that he was the person I had harassed. I had not realized that they had changed the sign at the intersection, so he was merely following the new rules. He laughed it off, but I felt foolish, and I felt like my stature had been diminished in my friend's eyes. My action had no chance to make me happy or money, and it had done the opposite.

Remember the Ace-Man's point. When you are considering doing something off-the-cuff or in anger, think, "will this make me money or happy?". If the answer is no, don't do it.

You shouldn't choose your friends based on how they impact your finances, but your friends should contribute to your happiness. If you have a friend that significantly negatively affects your finances, you should question if you have a co-dependent relationship that is probably hurting both of you.

Similarly, if you have relatives that are a persistent drain on your finances, you should look at the relationship. Of course, providing financial assistance to a loving parent that contributed to your success is an honorable and fair course to take. Providing support and guidance to younger relatives until they complete their education is also a commendable action to take (don't underestimate the importance of the guidance part).

Never loan a significant amount of money to a friend or relative. By significant, I mean an amount that would upset you if you didn't have it repaid. If a friend or relative asks you for a loan and you want to help them out, give them the money as a gift and tell them they can pay you back if they want to, but that it is a gift.

You must back up your words. If you don't get the money back, you cannot hold it against them. After all, it is a gift. Importantly, once someone close to you has been the beneficiary of such a gift, they are unlikely to ask for another gift. If they do and you don't want to give them any more freebies, that is your prerogative.

This method will tell you a lot about the character of those close to you. Good friendships and family relationships should not be torn apart by minor financial matters. Therefore, care should be taken to avoid this problem.

Similarly, if you are asked to co-sign a loan by a friend or relative, only do so if you are prepared to pay off the loan and have no hard feelings about it. Banks are in the business of making money on loans, so they like making loans. If they are not willing to make a loan to your friend or relative, it is because they realize there is a good chance the loan will not be repaid. You should have the same realization.

So far, I have discussed friends and relatives that can potentially harm your finances. But there is another side to this coin. Many of us have friends and relatives that can provide valuable financial advice, investments, and partnerships.

I didn't receive a lot of useful financial advice in my youth, but I have garnered a great deal of helpful financial advice from many of my friends since then.

After over a decade of unsuccessful dating, I heard the following advice, "never date someone with more problems than you." When I heard this, I realized that I had spent most of my single life dating women with more problems than me. I vowed to no longer date women that I perceived had more issues than me. I cannot put into words how much my dating life improved once I made this decision. In a very few years, I met my beautiful bride, and my life has improved steadily and often spectacularly since then. I am thankful that she didn't follow the same advice I did, but someone has to marry up.

I never made such a conscious decision regarding my friends' financial condition, but I did slowly migrate to hanging out with successful friends. It turns out that successful people are often engaging and delightful. Who knew? While we were having fun, I frequently asked their advice about all manner of things. They also picked my brain. It is called networking, and it is not an ugly word.

I know I always was delighted to put one of my friends in contact with another that could help them with a problem. Networking, when done correctly, is merely helping two friends or acquaintances to help each other. As a result, they are thankful to you. Networking is simply friends helping friends.

I found networking with successful friends to be advantageous, and I believe my friendship was beneficial to them. More than once, I helped a deserving friend get a job. It usually is a win-win situation.

It is a good idea to ask yourself if you are hanging around with winners. I don't advise cutting off ties with old friends that seem to be going nowhere in their careers or life (unless they become toxic). But you may need to move forward with your relationships.

There is an adage, "if you lay down with dogs, you will get fleas." In other words, if you consistently hang around with underachievers, it makes success more difficult. There is another adage, "success breeds success." This means that if you immerse yourself in successful surroundings with successful friends, you are more likely to achieve success.

Some adages are nonsense, but most are not. I believe that these two adages provide sound advice. If you want to move ahead in life, associate with successful people. If you consort with others solely for financial benefits, you are not acting with integrity, and you will probably soon be found out (I hope so).

The point is that you want to choose friends that will lift you up. Also, if there are friends that are dragging you down, you should reevaluate your relationship with them. The ideal friendship is one that helps both friends, financially and otherwise. It has been that way for millennia, and it is unlikely to change.

Chapter 3: Budget, Goals, and Debt

Make a Budget and Use It

If you don't save money, you will always be poor. I'll bet you didn't expect me to hit you with that one again. My daughters know that I can be annoyingly persistent with my advice when I think something is important. It is annoying, but they get it. I want you to get it too.

If you don't save money, you will always be poor.

So, how do you save money? It is difficult without planning, but if your expenses exceed your income, you *must* change something. But what? Fortunately, there is a tool that will help you to accomplish the goal of saving money. It's called a *budget*.

Oh no, not a budget! Most people don't like the idea of a budget because they view it as a restriction on their freewheeling lifestyle. Well, it can be that, but I think it is better to think of it as a plan that will lead to a better life.

Making a budget is hard enough, and sticking to it is harder still, but using a budget is a crucial component of financial success. Spending until there is no more to spend is easy. Therefore, spending and not budgeting is what most people do. That is why so many people have no savings.

If I go to the beach for a day with $50 in my pocket and no credit cards, I will probably spend $50. If I go to the beach with $30, I probably spend it all. If I go with $100, I am still probably going home with empty pockets or a few bucks. But, if I go to the beach with $100 and a $30 budget, I am likely to come home with $70. My values and wants don't change, but my behavior changes when I have a plan. This behavioral change is true of most people.

Having a plan (budget) and implementing it changes everything. The initial goal of a budget is simple: you want your income to exceed your expenses, and you want to invest the difference wisely.

It is confession time. I have spent a lot of time and words explaining to you how you absolutely, positively need to create a budget. Yet, I have never created and used a conventional budget. The reasons are simple. I am lazy, and budgets are a bit of a hassle, and I have found a substitute for the traditional budget that I prefer.

It is called a *reverse budget,* and it is not for everyone, but it can be a beneficial budgeting technique for many people. It has worked exceptionally well for me. I like the reverse budget because it takes minimal effort. Did I mention I'm lazy?

With a conventional budget, you pay all your bills first, and if you have planned well, you save or invest the leftover money. With a reverse budget, you make your savings or investments first, including savings for college, cars, house down payments, vacations, and retirement. After you save and invest, you pay all your bills.

If you are doing a reverse budget correctly, you will have some money left over after you save, invest, and pay your bills. You can use this money as "mad" money. In other words, use this money for whatever makes you happy. You can spend your mad money with the confidence of knowing you have taken care of the essential items of paying bills, saving, and investment. You can use mad money to have fun or to buy things you don't need, but that you want.

On the other hand, you can use mad money to pay down debts, increase investment, save more, or pay bills forward. Doing so will probably not win you the "Party Person of the Year" award. You probably were not going to win it anyway since I am pretty sure it doesn't exist. Still, taking these actions will make your life better.

Still, the point of reverse budgeting is that your money goes to the essential causes first, and you are free to have fun with the money left over. Reverse budgeting becomes very easy after you have set it up.

I use a simple rule of thumb with my reverse budgeting. I set a lower limit for our checking account, and I monitor our checking level to make sure it stays above the minimal level. If the account drifts down towards the minimum level, I know we must cut back on dinners at the steakhouse and replace them with burger runs, or, heaven forbid, make our food at home (the horrors). In other words, if the account is getting low, we tighten our belt. Simple enough.

On the other hand, if the checking account (where our mad money resides) grows to a level where we can comfortably take some cash out for some fun, we do so. Mad money can be used for vacations, concert tickets, gifts, and other luxuries. It can also be used for more mundane, but still rewarding things like making an investment or paying down the mortgage. Party on!

Either a reverse budget or a conventional budget will work if implemented correctly. In either case, you only have two options if your goals are not being met: earn more or spend less. If you don't take one of these options, you will not reach your goals. That's not cool.

If you choose to have a traditional budget, you must estimate your income and expenses. Most people want to make a monthly budget. I'd advise you to do this. It will require a little math. Oh no, say it isn't so! You can do a budget by hand, but it is easier to use Quicken software or a spreadsheet such as Microsoft's Excel. Mint (mint.com) also has budgeting and other financial management tools available for free. There are numerous other websites available that will also help with budgeting.

Most income and expense items can be translated into monthly values relatively easily. Other expenses are not so easy. For example, I pay my auto insurance bill of $1,200 every six months. It would be a big mistake not to include this expense in a monthly budget and then get hit with a surprise $1,200 bill in six months. Therefore, I should budget and put away $200 every month for this bill. After six months, I will have the $1,200. In any case, we mustn't forget about expenses that do not occur every month, such as vacations and home and car maintenance.

Similarly, we shouldn't forget about income that occurs less than once a month, such as an annual bonus. Your budget should not include income that you cannot depend on, such as an uncertain yearly bonus or a tax refund.

When you are estimating your income, it is best to be quite conservative by keeping your estimates of any uncertain income on the low side. That way, if there are any surprises, they will be pleasant surprises. In a like manner, you should estimate expenses on the higher end of the range in which you think they will fall. If you do so, most surprises will tend to be positive ones.

When estimating expenses, you start by breaking your expenses into categories. Common categories include housing (including maintenance, taxes, and insurance), food, clothing, healthcare (including gym memberships), transportation (including car payments, insurance, gas, and maintenance), phone, internet access, water & sewer, electric, natural gas, trash pick-up, charitable giving, entertainment, education (including student loans), personal care, and pet expenses.

Wow! That is a lot of categories, but I may have missed some. You will almost certainly have a category called "Miscellaneous" or "Other." There are nearly always some expenses that fall outside of the major categories.

An excellent way to create expense categories is to go over at least three months' worth of credit card statements and checking account statements and categorize every payment. If you use cash often, you should keep receipts for three months and categorize these payments. After you have categorized all your expenses for the past three months, creating an estimate of your expenses for the next year should become more manageable. Also, the process of categorizing past expenses can give you a good idea of areas that you are spending more money than is optimal for your financial well-being.

Another category that you should include is saving for future expenses (savings). You should have a separate category for each expense. If you want to take a vacation in Europe in two years, you should start saving today. If you have a ten-year-old car with 200,000 miles, you should start saving for your next car today (or more realistically when it had 100,000 miles). I have known many people that have complained about their decrepit car finally junking out for good and being dumbfounded at how they would deal with this *unexpected* expense. If you own a high ticket-value item that is nearing its expiration date, plan for the *cost* of replacing it long before it is likely to go to the vast junkyard in the sky.

If you don't have a checking account, you should get one as soon as you are financially able. Electronic deposits and payments save time and effort, and it is difficult to make electronic transactions without a checking account. Shop around for a checking account, factoring in convenience and cost. Once you choose a bank for your checking account, and then set up electronic transactions, it becomes a significant hassle to change banks. Therefore, you should put considerable thought into your bank choice.

If you have stable finances, it becomes easier to keep track of your expenditures and pay bills online. Also, automatic saving plans can be beneficial. If you have trouble saving money for the future, automatic saving plans can help to solve that problem. If you never see the money, it does not start to burn a hole in your pocket. The primary reason that I am currently much wealthier than I was in my twenties is that I started automatic saving plans, including a 401(k) in my twenties. I have the discipline now to save effectively manually, but automatic saving plans are just too easy and convenient to not use.

There is a caveat to automatically paying your expenses and automatically contributing to your savings. If you miscalculate and run out of money in your checking account, you can bounce payments and be hit with all sorts of expensive penalties and fees. Furthermore, this can inflict severe damage to your credit rating. Therefore, you must monitor your finances regularly (a few times a month).

In my youth, I bounced checks on two occasions. Both times, the problem resulted from income not being deposited in my account when as scheduled. So, it wasn't my fault. I didn't make a mistake. Guess what? No one cared. I still had to pay for all the fees and penalties. The system still pretty much works that way. Learn from my mistakes, and don't let this happen to you. It is unpleasant.

One thing you can do to help avoid problems like this is to balance your checkbook monthly and update it more often than that. I once had a close friend (that I may have married, but it would be unwise for me to reveal that information) that balanced her checkbook every month by simply writing in the balance on her monthly statement into her checkbook. She was fortunate that she never had any real problems with this method. She kept a relatively healthy balance, and that saved her from trouble, but she never really knew how much money she had. I convinced her that she should change her ways and balance her checkbook (perhaps by marrying her and doing it myself, maybe not, once again, protecting the innocent (myself)).

Balancing a checkbook can be challenging, especially if you do not write down transactions in a timely fashion. Once again, you can use computer tools such as Microsoft Excel to do the calculations for you. There are many websites on the web that can give you advice on how to balance a checkbook. Two such sites are:

nerdwallet.com/blog/banking/how-to-balance-a-checkbook/
emarquettebank.com/financial-education/articles-insights-for-you/eight-simple-steps-for-balancing-your-checkbook/

Websites are ever-changing, so if these sites don't work, search for "how to balance a checkbook" on the web, and numerous resources will appear.

If you don't learn how to manage a checking account first, it becomes much harder to manage the rest of your financial life. Take the time to effectively complete this vital step to managing your budget and achieving economic success.

Make Short-Term and Long-Term Goals and Measure Your Progress

An essential first step to financial planning is to create short-term and long-term goals. These goals don't have to be that complicated. Longer-term goals such as saving enough money to buy a house, saving for college for the kids, and being able to retire comfortably are essential. Short-term goals are also important because it is challenging to keep focused on goals for many years or even decades in the future. If we are achieving short-term goals that are improving our lives and creating a feeling of achievement, it is easier to continue making progress.

One possibility is to create goals that rid you of some of your worst financial problems. For example, pay off all my credit cards by a given date or move into a place I can afford that is close to my work. The latter goal comes from personal experience in my youth. I lost numerous jobs because I was not able to afford reliable transportation.

I joined the U.S. Army largely because of a lack of reliable transportation. If you have ever seen the start of the movie *Stripes* starring Bill Murray, you can get an accurate picture of how I joined the military. I was living in a trailer park with my Mother and four siblings, several miles outside of town. Sure, we were poor, but we had a double-wide, so, in a sense, the Joneses were trying to keep up with us.

A neighbor asked for a ride to his Mom's place. I told him that I didn't have enough gas to get back home or money for gas. He assured me that his Mom would compensate me with enough money that I could more than make it back home. He was incorrect. His mother was not there. He stayed, and I drove towards home, knowing that I had virtually no chance of making it back. I ran out of gas about 2 miles from home. There were no cell phones in those days, so I had to walk home and chisel some gas money out of my older brother.

My younger brother agreed to help me retrieve the car. Almost all vehicles today have fuel injection. That was not true then. Then, you had to prime the carburetor (pour some gas in the top of the engine) to start a car that had ran out of gas. My innocent younger brother poured too much gasoline, and when I started the engine, the top of the engine went up in flames. I, much like an action star, jumped out of my car, on to the roof, and then on to the hood of the vehicle, knocking it down to put out the fire…I thought. About 15 seconds later, the entire hood went up, and then most of the rest of the car.

Without a car, I couldn't drive to my work. Without work or a car, I lost my girlfriend. What's more, I had little prospect of a social life or a job because I was living in the sticks without any transportation. Hello, U.S. Army recruiter.

My descent into such a low point that I joined the military sounds like a sad story, but conversely, it was the beginning of the end of my poverty. My experience in the military was not as good as Bill Murray's. He had tons of laughs, saved western civilization, and started dating a girlfriend with movie-star good looks (go figure). Still, I vowed never again to have my life ruled by poverty, and I set short-term and long-term financial goals. The military gave me the discipline and a little bit of coin to begin to make my goals happen. Importantly, I read my first personal finance book during my military stint. I would never again live in poverty, and I started achieving my other goals.

It is a good idea to measure your progress towards your goals using the most commonly used measure of wealth, which is net worth. Net worth is the total value of your assets (house, car, investments, savings, and other things of monetary value) minus your debts (mortgage, car loans, credit cards, etc.) According to the U.S. Census Bureau, the median net worth of an American household was $80,000 in 2013. Is that a lot? Well, it depends.

A net worth of $80,000 sounds darn good if you are a 23-year old recent college graduate living in Tampa earning $90K a year with no kids. It is probably not so great if you are a 67-year old with no pension residing in New York City. The goodness of a net worth depends on many factors, including age, dependents, income, health, and financial goals.

If things are going well, your net worth should generally rise with age. There are exceptions. For example, my family's net worth went down during the period in my forties when I was earning my doctoral degree. I went from $80,000 to $20,000 a year in income for over five years while my wife was working part-time, and we had two kids, not exactly the recipe for financial success. Joyfully (sarcasm intended), the financial crisis of 2008 struck during the middle of my doctoral studies. That put a dent in our net worth. Still, we were sacrificing our short-term net worth for my increased future earnings and job satisfaction, so it worked out. Whew!

It is essential to calculate your net worth yearly to see if you are making progress. If your net worth goes down for a brief period for a good reason, such as going back to school, then that is probably okay if it is part of your plan. Still, you want to see steady progress toward your goals.

You calculate your net worth by subtracting your liabilities (debt) from your assets (things you can sell for money). You should value your assets at a price that you could sell them within a reasonable amount of time. Your letter jacket from high school or wedding pictures might be worth thousands of dollars to you, but they generally don't count as saleable assets unless you are Michael Jordan or Princess Kate. Don't worry about valuing your debts so much. The people that you owe money to will do an excellent job of that for you, and they tend to remind you of the exact amount of debt regularly.

There is a lot of great information and tools available on the internet that will help you to calculate your net worth. For example, Mint.com, BankRate.com, and CNN.com offer net worth calculators. Mint.com has the advantage of updating your net worth continuingly with little added input from you. You don't need to calculate your net worth precisely. It is more important that you calculate your net worth consistently yearly so that you can see your progress (or perish the thought, lack thereof) regularly.

I have found that if you can improve your life just a little each year, you are more likely to be happy. Enhancing your life slowly through your efforts seems to work much better at attaining happiness than winning a lot of money through the lottery. There is scientific research that backs my opinion up, but I am not going to cite it here, and I am going to reason that is because I want to keep this book short. Wow, avoiding work and making it seem logical. I've got skills.

If you increase your income, your net worth, and your financial security in most years, you are winning. Of course, increasing wealth should not be your only goal in life. It is okay if it is a primary goal. I know it has been one of mine for my adult life. Still, there needs to be a balance between pursuing wealth and enjoying life and between happiness today and happiness in the future.

If you use all your time and money to enjoy today, you will likely stay poor and not reach your financial or life goals. If you make a plan that will benefit you in the future, but that makes you miserable in the present, that plan is unlikely to work. Even if it does, you are still unhappy in the present. That stinks because you will never get that time back.

Research has shown that emotional intelligence can increase chances of success more than intelligence as measured by IQ tests. Once again, no citations in the name of brevity, *I'm killing it*. A key component of emotional intelligence is accepting delayed gratification. That means that you work and save today for future benefits. Earning an education is an example of delayed gratification. Certainly, financial success is much more likely if you accept delayed gratification. After all, saving for retirement is an ultimate form of delayed gratification in finance. Saving money for your benefit decades in the future is not easy, but it is a key to financial success.

We still believe that more intelligent people are more likely to succeed. Still, the ability to exercise deferred gratification is almost certainly more critical to financial success than simply being smart.

What is delayed gratification? I will explain it. Let's say that you love ice cream cones more than anything. In fact, ice cream cones are the only thing that matters to you. Let's say you can only purchase ice cream cones from me. I am the man.

Now, let's say I offer you a choice. You can either have:
   A) 2 cones this week and 0 next week (2 total)
                                       or
   B) 1 cone this week and 2 cones next week (3 total).

If you choose choice A, you are opting for immediate satisfaction. Gimme, gimme, I get it now. You are not delaying gratification. If you select choice B, you are delaying gratification. You only get one cone this week instead of two, but you get two next week for a total of three cones (more than the two cones of choice A). In this example, choice B is the obvious better choice if you love ice cream because you get more cones. That is unless you cannot delay gratification. If you have got to have the cones as soon as possible, you are hurting yourself because you are opting for fewer ice creams cones (the thing you love more than anything).

This ice cream cone example is straightforward, and the delayed gratification principle it teaches is a fundamental financial concept. In this example, all but the people that are most challenged by delayed gratification would choose choice B. Still, in real-world financial situations, the choice is not as obvious, and many people want instant gratification repeatedly.

That is what makes keeping to a budget such a problematic thing. Keeping a budget requires delaying gratification over and over with no certainty that the gratification will ever occur. Budgeting is quite literally saving money today that could benefit you today to benefit yourself in the future, perhaps decades in the future. That is not easy, but if you want to succeed financially, it is imperative to create and follow a budget.

Most of us have heard of the cliché of the middle-aged guy that buys a hot sports car to attempt to recapture his youth. There is probably a little bit of truth to the middle-age crisis cliché, but I have another theory. I believe many of those middle-aged guys saved their money for decades until they reached a point where they could comfortably spend the money on their dream car. I still haven't bought my dream car. So, I guess I will have an old-aged crisis at some point because I still want to own a vehicle that is entirely impractical, but fun. I believe it is coming soon. When it happens, I know I will have earned it because of my decades of budgeting and delayed gratification. Vroom!

The goal of budgeting should not be to only break-even every month. Your income should exceed your expenses by enough to reach your goals. First, you need goals. It is a good idea to set goals for one-year, five-years, ten-years, and retirement. Yes, you should think about retirement in your mid-twenties.

If you are financially intertwined with a significant other, you should work with them to agree on your shared goals. If you cannot formulate shared goals, you may need non-financial counseling. You should also put your goals in writing, signing in blood is optional.

Furthermore, you should begin preparing for your retirement in your twenties. This means you should start investing for something that is not going to happen for forty or fifty years or more. That is not intuitive or easy, but the old you will thank the young you if you do. The problem is that, for most people, the young self doesn't care or think very much about the old self. Don't let that be you. Your old self will thank you.

I'm getting up there in age, and I am very proud of the 27-year-old version of me. I thank that guy all the time for what he started for the old version of me. He was a great guy, prescient and quite the looker. Kudos to you, young me! You will want to thank your young self similarly.

Long-term goals are essential, but they are unlikely to be achieved if you do not set reasonable short-term goals. Very few of us can defer gratification for decades. Therefore, we must get smaller victories on the way to long-term financial security.

An excellent way to achieve these small victories is to set a series of short-term goals using the SMART technique. The goals should be:

S	specific
M	measurable
A	achievable
R	realistic
T	time-based.

Here are examples of a non-SMART and SMART goal. Non-SMART goal: "I want to solve my credit card problem." This is a noble goal, but it doesn't meet the smart criteria. Let's improve this goal to meet the SMART standards. SMART goal: "I want to pay off all of my credit cards within the next year. Furthermore, I want to keep them paid off monthly."

This goal is specific, measurable, and time-based. It can also be achievable and realistic, depending on your circumstances.

The achievable and realistic goals can depend on many factors. You want to achieve your financial goals as quickly as possible without overly sacrificing present happiness. Just like your long-term goals, you should put your short-term goals in writing and share them with others you trust. This will give you extra motivation to achieve your goals.

Creating goals is necessary to keep you on track. The idea that you have important goals will help you when you are forgoing small pleasures. Soon, you may not miss some of the little joys that you have foregone or replaced with more affordable desires. You will undoubtedly notice the disappearance of the accompanying financial stress that repeated small pleasures and poor budgeting create. Remember, saving five dollars a day equals saving $1,825 a year.

During your first year on a budget, you should review your budget, short-term goals, and long-term goals monthly. After the first year, you only need to consider your short-term goals and budget every month. You should still review your long-term goals every three months. Please note that reviewing your finances does not need to be a significant time-consuming event. It can take anywhere from a few minutes to one or two hours but should not take longer unless you are making substantial revisions.

Reviewing goals regularly is vital because adjustments to your goals and budget will almost certainly be necessary. If you are one of the rare people that gets your goals and budget correct on the first try, adjustments will still need to be made as your finances, personal life, and goals change.

If you are not meeting your goals, you must adjust your budget or find a way to make more income. Another option is to lower your goals, though that is rarely satisfying if you started with realistic goals. If you are meeting or exceeding your goals, you can keep on doing what you are doing and celebrate your success. You also have the option of raising your goals, but remember that it is okay to enjoy life if you are making the financial progress that you want to achieve.

If you have set up your budget and goals correctly and made proper adjustments as time goes on, your finances should improve steadily. If you have a significant, unplanned problem such as extreme medical problems or a severe accident, progress could be halted, and short-term goals and budgets may have to be redone. If the problems are not permanent, long-term goals may remain mostly intact.

You mustn't give up on financially planning if you face significant problems. Financial planning will become more critical than before. One of the primary goals of financial planning is to get to the point where one can handle major problems without incurring financial disaster. It may take a few years to get to the position where one can weather a major financial emergency, but emergencies are likely to happen eventually. Therefore, preparing for these problems is essential.

Life becomes more pleasant if your finances are improving even if you are doing less and buying less. The presence of financial security and the absence of financial stress will have an overwhelmingly positive impact on your life. Once your investments are making more, and your debt is reduced, you will be able to do and buy more in the long run with less stress. Money can't buy happiness, but it does make it more likely.

It is important to note that you will not automatically be happier once your finances improve. You need to make wise decisions in other aspects of your life. You may require psychological counseling. Once I became "not poor," I became confused. I had always thought that my financial situation was the primary reason I was unhappy. It was a reason, but there were others. After a series of bad decisions related to my love life and my career, I got some counseling and started making better non-financial decisions. Over the last two-plus decades, I would describe myself as a happy person, not every day, of course, but happy. That is, after all, the primary goal. A good financial situation is a crucial part of achieving this goal, but it is by no means the only thing.

There is a Buddhist philosophy that states that "pain is caused by desire." I am not Buddhist, but I have done some reading on the subject, and I believe some Buddhist teachings can benefit anyone.

For example, I still use a technique I learned from my readings about Buddhist philosophy to help myself fall asleep. FYI, I concentrate on my breathing and try to ignore all other thoughts. It works for me. Try it if you have trouble sleeping. It takes a little practice, but getting a good night's sleep can also improve your finances.

Back to the philosophy that "pain is caused by desire." If this is true, then if you manage to desire less, you will be happier and experience less pain. Can you be happier if you spend less on entertainment, food, utilities, and rent or mortgage? It certainly is an idea worth exploring. We all know that many people of modest means are much happier than many extremely wealthy people. A simple way to improve your finances is to lower your desire for things, especially expensive items.

So now, you have short-term and long-term goals, a budget, and a balanced checkbook — Pat yourself on the back. Metaphorically, I mean. I don't want you to pull a muscle or something, that would increase your healthcare costs and bust your new budget. Most people do not have these four financial tools in place. Most of them are not on the right road, you are.

It is essential not to get discouraged in the early going. The goal is to make progress towards your goals. Slow progress is okay; faster progress is better. If you are making progress, you can adjust your finances to increase your progress or increase your financial satisfaction.

You will be able to make faster progress if you do not buy unnecessary luxuries that you must maintain. Expensive cars, electronics, jewelry, and other non-necessities may require maintenance and insurance and incur additional costs in time and money.

If you have some expensive items you would like to resell, remember that you should never consider sunk costs. Sunk costs should not be considered in any financial decision. What are sunk costs? That is money that you have spent that you will not get back no matter what decision you make. Many people make decisions based on sunk costs because psychologically, it is difficult not to want to recover money that we have lost or wasted. Still, sunk costs are, by definition, sunk, gone, *finito*.

Here is an example of a poor decision based on sunk costs that was made by someone I know, but *definitely* not by me. I, I mean, this hypothetical person, was planning to trade his beat-up jalopy in for a newer model within a few days. Unfortunately, the piece-of-schadenfreude car broke down the day before it was scheduled to be traded and required about $1,000 of repairs. The repairs had to be made before the vehicle could even be driven to be traded.

This unfortunate, hypothetical person happened to be at one of my kid's birthday parties and he complained about his bad luck and stated to one of my good friends (who happened to be an astute business person) that now he had to keep driving the car that he had come to despise for another few months so that he could recover the money he had just put into the car. My friend simply stated: "Sunk costs. You have already spent the money, and you are not going to get it back by driving the car longer. Something else may break, and then you will have to spend more money on that jalopy." I, I mean this hypothetical person that just happened to be at my party talking to my friend about…okay, it was me; realized that I had made a classic financial mistake.

I had failed to ignore my sunk costs. I was not going to get back the car repair money no matter what I did. I decided to follow my friend's sound advice, and I traded the car in the next day. It felt so good to get rid of that heap. Another way to look at failing to ignore sunk costs is that you are "throwing good money after bad." I think we all know not to do that. You should ignore sunk costs (money you cannot get back). To do otherwise is irrational and wasteful.

Back to deferring luxuries until you are already wealthy. Robert T. Kiyosaki says in his iconic book *Rich Dad Poor Dad*, that "rich people buy luxuries last, while the poor and middle class tend to buy luxuries first."

I don't agree with everything Kiyosaki writes in his book (then again, he is way wealthier than me), but I absolutely agree with him on this point. I have seen scores of friends, relatives, and acquaintances start to succeed financially and then blow thousands of dollars on cars, vacations, and other luxuries. Before too long, they end up right back where they started because they didn't invest their excess money, they spent it instead.

I have two good long-time friends that have had successful construction businesses for decades. The construction business is notoriously cyclical, good times are followed by bad times followed by good times and on and on. My friends have noticed that many of their peers take out mortgages and car loans and spend money on exotic vacations and other luxuries when times are good. When things go wrong, they cannot pay their bills, and they go bankrupt. My friends save when times are good, and they are glad of it when times are bad.

Another downside to owning lots of things, including luxuries, is that these items don't only take money to maintain, but they also take time. At some point, it seems more like your things own you and not the other way around. A few years back, I read about a wealthy man that vowed only to own 100 items. A silverware set did not represent an item, a fork did. This plan seemed to be working very well for this man, and he was exuberant about the amount of free time he had to do what he wanted. He could make more money or do something fun. It was his choice.

His lifestyle was somewhat extreme. I couldn't talk my wife into a similar lifestyle, and I am not sure I wanted to do so. Still, I think most of us could improve our life by moving closer to the simple lifestyle this person was leading. Imagine if you didn't have to clean, maintain, rearrange, sort through, and pay for storage for so many things. I believe it is something to consider.

We have adopted a policy that if we haven't used an item in the last year and we are unlikely to use it in the next year, we should get rid of it (unless we can make a strong argument why we should not dump it). We have downsized our possessions a great deal following this policy, but we certainly have room for improvement. If you follow a similar strategy, you might be able to save on all kinds of expenses. After all, how much does a storage unit cost, and how many of us really need what is in the storage unit? If we needed it, would it be in there?

If you are making progress on your short-term and long-term goals, you are on the road to getting rich slowly. That is a much better result than staying poor consistently.

Avoid Debt

Credit cards are wonderful. Credit cards are terrible. It depends on how you use them. It is better to not use credit cards at all than to misuse them. So, let's learn how to use them properly.

Here is the most important rule about using credit cards: ***Pay your credit card balances in full every month***. If you do this, you will not have to pay any interest on your credit card purchases. If you have a credit card that requires you to pay interest when you pay the entire balance every month, you have the wrong credit card.

This brings up an important point about credit cards. Their terms vary a great deal. Most give grace periods in which you do not have to pay interest if you pay the card off before the grace period ends. Some charge annual fees, while many do not. Interest rates vary wildly, but they are almost always higher than any other type of loan you may receive (except for payday loans, loans at check-cashing stores, and pawn shops). There are usually substantial financial penalties if you make a payment late. Many cards offer points that can be used to get free flights, hotels, and other benefits. Similarly, many cards offer cash back on purchases.

I recommend cards that have a grace period, no annual fees, and that offer cash back on purchases. Points may be preferable to some people in certain situations, but I like the money. It is easier to understand than calculating points, and it is, well, cash. Who doesn't want some money? If you pay your credit card off on time every month, the grace period means that the credit card company is essentially giving you an interest-free loan equal to around 40 days. Sweet! If you pay your credit card off every month as you should, the interest rate and late fees become less important.

Now, here comes a problem for many people. If you have bad credit, you may not qualify for the best credit cards. You may have to pay an annual fee. You may have to accept a higher interest rate. You may not be able to get a cash-back or points reward card. If not, get the best card you can and pay it off every month on time. If you do this, you should soon be able to get a better credit card that offers better terms.

Many young people or people that have had credit problems want to know how to build their credit. There is no big secret. ***The best way to build credit is to pay off all your bills on time every time***. There are other smaller things you can do to build credit, but this is the best way by far.

Your credit score will be based on factors similar to your FICO® Score. Your FICO® Score considers five categories of credit data from your credit report that may vary in importance for different credit profiles. The percentages vary over time, but you can view the following category percentages a rough estimate of the significance of the categories to your credit rating: payment history (35%), amount you owe (30%), length of credit history (15%), new credit opened (10%), types of credit (10%). Once again, the best way to build credit is to pay off all your bills on time every time.

You may be able to get credit cards from retailers before you can get credit cards from Visa, MasterCard, American Express, or Discovery. These cards can be used to build credit if you pay them off on time. Once again, you do not want to carry a balance and incur interest costs.

A great website to use when trying to find a credit card to meet your needs is bankrate.com (bankrate.com). There are other useful websites available, but this is one that I have used to research credit cards, auto loans, certificates of deposit (CD), and mortgage rates, and I highly recommend it.

Once you can qualify for major credit cards (Visa, MasterCard, American Express, or Discovery), you should have three major credit cards. At least one of these cards should be either Visa or MasterCard because numerous businesses do not accept American Express or Discovery). It is essential to have more than one card because you need a backup in case your primary card is compromised (through fraud or some other method).

Over the last ten years, my wife and I have had one of our cards compromised on several occasions through no fault of our own. On these occasions, it was convenient to have two other cards to use until we got our new cards to replace the compromised cards.

Also, you should cancel your retail cards once you have major credit cards. It makes managing your credit much more manageable and reduces your chances of becoming a victim of fraud.

Are cash rewards cards that rewarding? You bet your sweet bippy (Google that)! I have had a cash rewards card for over 20 years, and I have collected over $15,000 in rewards so far. Cash rewards cards are becoming more rewarding, and my wife and I have received well over $1,000 a year over the last few years.

We currently have three credit cards. One pays 5% in cash rewards for gasoline purchases, 3% rewards for dining and travel, and 1% cash rewards for everything else. We use this card for gasoline, dining, and travel. Another card pays 2% cash back on everything. We use this card for everything but gasoline, dining, and travel. Our third card pays 1 ½ % cash back, and we rarely use it, but it provides a good emergency card. It takes a small amount of effort to manage our three cards, but the cash back rewards are amazing. We are on a path to receive over $2,000 in rewards this year. Why would anyone that qualifies for such rewards pass them up? I don't know, but some do.

Now, cash rewards cards are not a good idea if you don't pay your bill in full every month. Interest charges can more than offset cash rewards. Also, if you buy things you usually wouldn't buy to receive cash rewards, that is just crazy. Once again, the key is to pay off your credit cards every month.

Misuse of credit cards is one of the most common causes of bankruptcy. Credit card companies don't want you to go bankrupt because that hurts them if you owe them money. But, if you're going to pay a high credit card interest rate on your balance year after year, they are okay with that. Unfortunately, if you are carrying a high level of debt and something goes wrong to disrupt your finances severely, you may not be able to pay your debts, and everyone loses — simple solution: pay of your entire credit card balance every month.

As I am writing this book, the average credit card interest rate is 13% (many cards have substantially higher rates). This average rate of 13% is historically quite low, so it is likely to go up in the future. The average credit card balance is $1,000. That means that the average person pays $130 in interest per credit card per year. Many people have several credit cards, so the average credit card interest paid per person is even more substantial. This goes on for a lifetime for some people.

What do these people get for carrying credit card debt and paying hundreds or thousands of dollars year after year? Almost nothing. They don't get anything more than they would have had without the debt. They just get some stuff sooner when they first go into debt. After that, they must reduce their consumption by the amount of interest they are paying every month. In other words, they get less stuff until they pay the debt off.

Don't make the mistake of merely paying the minimum payment amount. If you do that, you are almost guaranteeing that you will be paying a high-interest rate on a high balance for many years. As a practical matter, people that routinely pay the minimum payment, never pay off their credit card debt. Never!

Don't be fooled by teaser rates offered for new credit cards or credit card debt transfers. These sound like good deals, but they usually aren't. You may be offered a 0% interest rate on a new card or a transfer of debt from another card (with a substantial fee), but these rates are usually very short-term (six-months or less). The problem is that most people take the teaser rate, keep a high balance on the card, don't pay the card off at the end of the teaser-rate period, and then start paying high-interest rates again.

Zero percent interest rates sound too good to be true. Well, they usually are. How can the credit card company make money if they are charging 0% interest? They cannot unless they make money somewhere else.

You should check your credit card account regularly, at least once a month. I recommend checking it more often online or setting up your account so that you are notified on your phone when purchases are made using your card. If you check your account more often, it is much easier to detect fraud or bogus charges. Credit card fraud is common, and it is a hassle when you are targeted, but it becomes less of a hassle the sooner you notice the problem.

Once you have a credit card, I recommend that you do *not* use a debit card. If you have a checking account and you like using an ATM occasionally, this is difficult to do. Every time that I have received a new ATM card in the last 15 years, the bank has sent me a debit card. I then must contact them to have the card changed to an ATM only card, not a debit card.

Why do I prefer not to have a debit card? The reason is that I don't want to shoulder the risk associated with a debit card. Also, I have never used a debit card for anything other than accessing an ATM. In comparison to a credit card, a debit card has enormous risks associated with it.

If you lose a credit card and report it within a reasonable amount of time (usually two days), your potential loss is limited to $50. Typically, if your credit card number is stolen and used to make purchases, your damage is zero. I have had my credit card number stolen over five times, and it has caused me considerable aggravation, but it has not cost me a penny.

If you have your debit card stolen, the thieves may empty your bank account before you know they have done so. If you are innocent of any wrongdoing or gross incompetence, you will *probably* get all your money back *eventually*. In the meantime, you may not have any money for an extended period. This can negatively affect your relationship with those that you owe money, and they may assess you penalties for paying late. Yuck!

The banks behind the three credit cards I currently hold offer me a free credit report and FICO score quote every year. This leads me to believe that most credit cards now offer this service for free. You should not have to pay for a credit report or credit score because they are available for free.

Every year, you can request one free credit report from each of the three major credit agencies (Equifax, TransUnion, and Experian). The easiest way to request free credit reports is to visit AnnualCreditReport.com. Other websites claim to offer free credit reports. They may even have "free" in their name, but they usually have caveats and exceptions that will end up separating you from your money. I'd advise sticking with AnnualCreditReport.com.

If you have a credit card, your credit card company is probably trying to sell you credit life and disability insurance. These are insurance policies that will pay off your credit card balance if major misfortune or debt befalls you. These are usually a terrible deal. If you want disability or life insurance (not a bad idea), purchase them elsewhere. When these types of policies are associated with a credit card, they benefit the company selling them enormously. First, they are selling you significantly overpriced insurance, thus ensuring a sizable profit. Secondly, if the insurance policy pays off, it benefits the card company most of all, because your balance gets paid off despite your suddenly dire circumstances. You will likely still be in dire circumstances unless you have other more comprehensive and less expensive insurance.

If you have severe credit card or other debt problems, there are counselors available that can help you to work out a debt repayment plan. It is better to seek help before your problems become intractable. You can find support from The National Foundation for Consumer Credit

(NFCC) (nfcc.org), American Consumer Credit Counseling (consumercredit.com), InCharge Institute of America (incharge.org), Money Management International (moneymanagement.org) and Dave Ramsey (daveramsey.com).

Chapter 4: Reduce Expenses

Make Saving a Habit

If you don't save money, you will always be poor.

Remember that one, it is still valid. Of course, saving money is not that easy. Spending is so much more fun…in the short-term. In the long-term, if you spend all you make (or more than you make), you will always be poor.

Saving money on smaller purchases may seem relatively unimportant, but to quote Bruce Springsteen, "from small things, Mama, big things one day come." Making smart decisions on everyday purchases can result in yearly savings in the hundreds or even thousands of dollars.

Through the years, I have seen dozens of stories in the news of a factory or business shutting down where they interview a person that has been working at the closing company for decades. I've never seen them interview a person that has been preparing for this situation for years, and they think they will be just fine.

They interview someone that has been working there for decades, and they have no idea how they are going to pay next month's bills. I marvel at the person that has a steady job for decades and yet has no savings or plans for what they are going to do after they lose their job. If you are ever in a similar situation, you want to be the person they don't interview.

Job one, when planning to save, is to make a budget and stick to it. We covered that earlier. Also, you should be searching for ways to save money regularly. I often find great tips in news and articles that I find on the internet because I am interested in learning how to save some money or make extra money easily. Sometimes friends or even an advertisement (be careful though) provide useful ideas on how to save money. The important thing is to be open to ideas and search for new ones. Some ideas that I have discovered through the years follow.

A key to saving is exercising self-discipline. You need to create a plan and stick with it. Only change the plan to improve it. Do not change the plan so that you can backslide into not saving. If you keep your focus on doing well in the short-term by sticking to your plan, you will see the benefits, sometimes huge benefits, in the long-term.

Keep your expenses low. Earn as much income as you can without ruining your life. Save or invest the difference wisely. Pay attention to your savings. You need to keep your emergency savings in a safe account, preferably an FDIC-insured account at a bank. Savings or investments not tagged for emergencies should earn higher returns elsewhere. If you do these things, you should be able to buy that dream home or fun car in the future without the stress of worrying about financial security.

Making more money can be difficult. If it weren't, you would already be making more money. Saving money can be easier than making more money. It can be easy not to buy something or buy something less expensive than another item you are considering.

Also, if you decide not to buy a one-dollar item, let's make it a hamburger (or veggie burger, your choice), you save the whole dollar. Even better, you are saving a dollar plus sales tax. That is $1.07 in my town, and, frankly, it wouldn't hurt me to forego a few burgers. On the other hand, if I wanted to earn a dollar more, I'd have to make more than a dollar. The reason I would have to earn more than a dollar is that I'd have to earn enough to pay the income tax and any work-related expenses such as transportation. So, for example, I might have to earn $1.40 or $1.50 or more to earn that dollar after taxes and expenses. It does make saving a dollar instead look better.

Let's look at an example where a small consumer choice change can make a significant change in savings over the long-term. I will choose a topic I have a passing knowledge of, beer. If you are a teetotaler, you can apply this example to many other consumer items. Let's say I like to have two beers each night, five nights a week at a local pub. That's ten beers a week, nice round number that. Let's say that I don't drink at all four weeks a year. That works out to 48 weeks a year of drinking ten beers a week. The grand total is 480 beers a year. The number 480 is evenly divisible by six, so maybe you see where I am going with this.

At the local pub, I could buy two premium import beers for $7 (including tip) each or two domestic beers for $5 (including tip) each. Those living in New York City are probably laughing at these ludicrously low prices about now. But these are realistic prices in much of the country, and we often can do better during happy hour and with drink specials. So, who's laughing now?

There are other options, though. Let's say I would just as soon drink a couple of brews with my neighbor or my brother. Now, if I buy the beer in six-packs (cases might be even cheaper), let's say the import now costs $2 a pop, and the domestic costs $1 per brew. Well, that's better.

How does the math work out for my different options? For the import at the pub, I am looking at a yearly bill of $3,360. Does this number shock you? It shocks me, and I am writing this book. The domestic beer at the pub works out to $2,400. That is still a lot to pay annually, but it is almost a thousand-dollar savings *every year* versus the import. I started drinking beer when I was in the U.S. Army and stationed in Germany. So I appreciate a quality import as much as anyone, but that kind of savings make me want to buy American.

But wait, there is more. What about the hanging with friends' options? Well, the import option comes in at $960, and the low-cost winner at $480 is drinking the domestic with friends. Drinking the import at home saves $2,400 compared to drinking the import at the pub. Drinking the domestic brew at home saves almost three thousand dollars ($2,880 to be exact).

It is important to note that these savings are calculated on an *annual* basis. The savings over the longer-term would be much more significant. For example, the import at home versus the import at the pub would save $120,000 over 50 years. That is not a typo, and my math is impeccable. You may say that my calculations do not take inflation into account, and you would be correct, but including an inflation adjustment only increases the savings.

You may like going to the pub, have a crush on the bartender, and think the servers are smoking hot. Also, you might love the import and think the American brew is swill. That's okay. If you greatly value the comradery available at the pub and you want to keep drinking the good stuff, that is fine. But now you know what it costs you, and if you can't save money elsewhere, you know this is a place to save money. If you want to save money, you can drop the beer and take up tap water (I know, I know, I'm not doing that either). Still, cutting back on vices is not only good for you, but it will save you money.

The important thing about this line of considering saving options is that you discover your options and what each option costs you annually. You should think of all your recurring expenses this way. If you do so, you will learn of all your saving opportunities and be able to make informed choices.

We have covered the essential points of setting goals and budgeting already, but the little things are a necessary component of success in sticking to a budget. After all, if you can either save or make a little bit more daily, your finances will change a great deal over the long-term. For example, if you either save or make (after tax) $2.75 more a day, that works out to a $1,000 difference over a year. Small changes in behavior can make significant differences over the long-term. Therefore, you should regularly be looking for opportunities to improve your every day or every-month financial decisions. Frequently, these decisions can improve your financial situation significantly with no significant effect on the benefit your dollars spent garner you.

Anytime that you borrow money, remember to shop around for a loan with the lowest interest rate and fees. A great place to shop for the best interest rates on automobile loans, mortgages, credit cards, and other loans is bankrate.com. It is also a great place to shop for checking and savings accounts and CD rates. A small change in interest rates can make a big difference in money spent or earned over the long-term. It is a great idea to focus on the long-term.

Bankrate.com is not the only good website to use to shop for loans and bank accounts, but it is a very good one. Also, it is important to remember that most loans, like many investments, are sold. That means that you may often get a high-pressure approach from a salesperson to borrow from them on their terms. Often, they tell you that their deal is far better than any other deal you will get out there. This is unlikely to be accurate and is a good signal that you should be very wary of the salesperson pitching this loan. Avoid high-pressure sales on all items, including loans.

You should have a checking account and a savings account. You should shop for financial services that have the lowest fees. Also, if you need to borrow money, shop for the lowest interest rates. Join a credit union. Regulations for banks and credit unions differ, and so do the prices and interest rates for services they provide. If you are in a credit union, you can use it when it benefits you. The difference between the rates of different institutions can be substantial. These differences can result in differences in your wealth of hundreds of dollars a year.

Remember, there is no such thing as "free financing." If you are offered an interest rate of zero percent, you should be wary. You may be overpaying for what your buying. This may be a teaser rate that explodes to a much higher rate if you do not pay everything off by a pre-specified date. Sometimes it is a good idea to accept a below-market financing rate. You need to know precisely why you can get this great deal.

If you are considering a purchase or investment, and it sounds too good to be true, please be extremely cautious. If someone is urging you to jump on this opportunity before it goes away, you should be afraid (especially if that person is receiving a commission or otherwise benefits from this fantastic opportunity *for you*). My advice to you in these situations is the same advice given in the movie *Monty Python and the Holy Grail*, "run away, run away!"

Using your time to shop around for any recurring expense such as home insurance, car insurance, apartments, internet service, phone service, and gym memberships is time well spent. Recurring expense items can be budget-busters or budget-makers. Again, annualize the amount spent on these types of things so that you can see the full impact. A difference of $75 a month in rent doesn't sound that big, but a difference of $900 a year does even though they are the same thing.

The internet has made comparing prices remarkably easy. Some things are difficult to shop for on the internet. I have not had a great deal of luck with shoes or clothing that I have not tried on or purchased before. But I have gotten great deals on running shoes from my favorite brand and underwear brands I already own.

There is a particular brand of sport earbuds that I go through regularly because I am rough on them while exercising. I have never found these buds for less than $20 in stores, but I can get them for less than $15 online. Therefore, I have learned to buy them ahead of time so that they will be ready the next time I break my old ones. It is only a $5 difference, but I go through about three a year. I don't know about you, but I would pick up $15 if I found it lying on the sidewalk. A little bit of planning saves me that much a year on just this one item.

Planning is a crucial component of being an accomplished online shopper. If you regularly shop on Amazon, Amazon Prime is well worth it. Paying extra for faster shipping can significantly reduce savings. I have paid extra for expedited shipping for holiday or birthday gifts. When this has happened, frugal me has harshly ridiculed procrastinating me and with good reason. I have become much better in recent years at avoiding extra shipping costs. This has resulted in inner harmony.

Planning is also a good idea for shopping in traditional stores. Generally, you should avoid impulse buys. If you see something on sale in a store that you were planning to buy soon anyway, go ahead and buy it. If something is a good deal, but you weren't planning to buy it, and you don't need it, don't get it. In this case, you are not saving money. You are spending money unnecessarily.

Avoiding extra trips to the store is a worthy goal that saves money and time. Buying things that you need in bulk can often facilitate fewer trips to the store. Check the price per unit, such as price per ounce, to be sure you are saving money. Joining a warehouse club can be worth the price if you can shop there regularly.

Shopping at discount stores is an option that should be considered. Look for sales on items you purchase regularly and stock up when they go on sale. Consider buying store brands. Often, they are the same or better quality than branded products. Sometimes, they are not. Live and learn.

Sometimes, you may be given the option to pay for a good or service immediately or make payments over time. In these cases, it is usually preferable to pay the entire bill upfront if you can garner a substantial discount for doing so.

If you find coupons for items you purchase anyway, use them. I used to clip coupons for all sorts of grocery items, but I eventually determined it was not a good use of my time. Still, if you enjoy clipping coupons, have fun. If local charities, such as schools, offer discount cards to local businesses, those are often a great value. You help a worthy charity and save money. What's not to like?

Frequent restaurants you enjoy on nights when they have exclusive deals. Using apps for restaurants and stores that you frequent can result in substantial savings. I frequent three restaurants where my app for those establishments entitles me to a ten-dollar discount for every $200 spent. That is found money.

Don't overspend on gifts. Would you want your friends and love ones to bust their budgets on gifts for you? If you genuinely have good friends and loving loved ones, they will not want you to strain your resources for their gifts. Often, time together is the greatest gift. It is also a low-cost gift. Indeed, it is the thought that counts.

Utilities are recurring expenses. Electricity, natural gas, gasoline, and water are a significant expense for most people. Sometimes, it is a good idea to spend some money upfront to save money in the long run. Buying more energy-efficient appliances, water-saving devices (such as a rain barrel), and reducing driving or driving a more energy-efficient vehicle can result in critical recurring savings.

When you are making a significant purchase, do some research on what you are buying. The magazine and website *Consumer Reports* (consumerreports.org) is a reliable resource for product ratings and reviews. They accept no advertising dollars because advertising revenue concerns can significantly bias reviews of products. Therefore, you should take the reviews of any source that allows advertising with a grain of salt. Most libraries have subscriptions to *Consumer Reports,* so you do not necessarily need to subscribe to their magazine or website to use their service. Of course, there are numerous other resources on the web, attempt to make sure you are not relying on biased information.

I want you to save your money, but there are some crucial areas where you should not skimp. One of these areas is safety and security. Don't drive an unsafe car and don't live in an area that is unsafe if you can avoid it.

Pay for a home security system, even if you are renting. There are portable systems now available, such as SimpliSafe (simplisafe.com), that will get the job done that you can take with you once you move. Put up the warning signs that the security system protects your home. Most criminals prefer not to wrangle with a security system, so if you warn them that you have one, they are more likely to avoid your residence. A security system will help to protect your belongings, but more importantly, it will help to protect you and your loved ones. You can buy more stuff, but you often can't get back what you lose when you are physically harmed.

Quitting or cutting back on vices is a beautiful way to save money. You can rarely save money while improving your life. Omitting vices is one such way. All four of my siblings have smoked in the past, and I think all of them are currently smoking. I don't know because periodically, one of them will try to quit, and they have had some limited success for months in the past. I do know that if my siblings had saved the money that they spent on smoking, they would have enough money to buy a quaint country cottage today. A house, they could buy a house! If they chose to spend their cigarette money individually, they could all afford to buy new cars of varying quality today.

I've never smoked, but I have my vices. Oh, I could save a few hundred dollars a year if I didn't drink diet sodas. I could save over a thousand dollars a year if I didn't enjoy beer so much. I blame my stint in Germany with the Army for my lust for quality malted beverages. Still, I search for opportunities to save money on these items, stocking up on my favorites when they are on sale. Sometimes, I trade down to cheaper brands. I avoid paying up in restaurants when possible because diet sodas and beer are both much more affordable at the grocery store. I even brewed beer at home for a few years, and I will probably do so again when I retire. The point is that if you are not going to quit your vice, cut back and save as much as possible while continuing your wicked ways ☺.

Pets bring great joy to most people, but pets are a significant expense. Their food isn't cheap. They need medical care that can be unpredictable. Most people must pay someone to care for their pets when they go out of town. If you are a renter, you usually must pay a sizable deposit, often non-refundable, to own a pet. If you are a homeowner, you usually must pay for things the pet destroys or defaces. Those are just some of the downsides to owning a pet.

Now, for some of the upsides. They are so cute! We love them! That is pretty much it, but those are biggies.

Still, you should always consider the total cost of pet ownership when you make the big decision to have a pet. You should also be mindful that many pets become considerably more expensive as they age. We had a cat that had medical costs of over $100 a month for the last five years of her life. For you home gamers, that is $6,000 total. That is what I mean by *significant expense.*

Furthermore, it became an expense that we could not avoid. That old cat was my wife's baby, and the kitty would even cuddle me when Mom was not available. Any port in a storm from the cat's point of view. I would not advise anyone that genuinely wants one not to get a pet. I would encourage you to realize the economic effect of that decision fully.

Vacations, especially family vacations, are essential. Vacations are times to recharge the batteries, relax, enjoy, and build memories. If done correctly, vacations should be the best part of your year. That said, it is foolish to mortgage your future to enjoy a few weeks a year. Vacations should not be something that causes one to lose their home, go into crushing debt, lose educational opportunities, risk a comfortable retirement, or endure bankruptcy. Yes, vacation choices are often a significant contributor to people going bankrupt. Crazy, no?

It is easy to overspend on vacations. It is smart to avoid doing so. The main goals of vacations are fun and relaxation. But, if a vacation strains your finances so much that you have less fun and are stressed out the rest of the year, mission not accomplished. Most people can find enjoyable and relaxing vacation options that don't have high costs. It is worth the effort.

So, plan reasonable vacations that you can afford. A week at a local lake in an affordable hotel or camping site is not nearly as cool as a week at The Four Seasons on the Riviera, but it can be as much fun, will probably be more relaxing and will cost a fraction of the more exotic vacation. If you do travel overseas, use a credit card or your bank ATM card to get a reasonable exchange rate for foreign currency.

When planning a trip, hit the internet to get discounts on hotels, cars, and flights. There is no shortage of websites in this business. I usually start at Priceline, but that is because I know how to work it the best. I typically check many other sites as well. It is not unusual to save 50% or so off the listed price, certainly worth the effort.

Try to stretch your vacation dollar as far as possible. Travel during non-peak seasons for your destination. If you are flexible about your travel dates, you can usually save a lot of money. Use discount travel websites such as Kayak (kayak.com), Priceline (priceline.com), and Hotwire (hotwire.com). I use Priceline most often because I have learned how to navigate it well. It doesn't always save me money on all my trips, but sometimes it saves me hundreds of dollars. It doesn't take long to use one or more of these or similar websites. The substantial potential savings make it worthwhile.

If you are ever offered a free prize or vacation in return for sitting through a vacation timeshare presentation, I'd highly advise you not to do it. The purveyors of these offers are expert at getting people to buy timeshares that they had no intention of buying. Most of these timeshares end up being more expensive than merely vacationing at the same spot year after year.

High upfront costs and recurring fees usually make the long-term value of a timeshare exorbitant. Often, you have little control over the increase of annual fees, and the fees must be paid whether you use the timeshare or not. Most timeshare resales go for a fraction of the original price. This should tell you something about the value of a new timeshare. Timeshares almost certainly go down in value by a substantial amount. Just say no to timeshares.

If you get the urge to purchase a vacation property, be cautious. It really doesn't make sense unless you are already wealthy and plan to spend several months a year at the vacation property. The cost of maintenance and security when you are not at the property can be high. Renting out the property can also be problematic.

Vacations are an essential part of enjoying life, but they also can be a significant expense. Good decisions on the balance between enjoyable vacations and smart spending on them can improve your quality of life.

Warehouse clubs such as Costco, B.J.s, and Sam's Club are often worth joining, especially if they are located near you, and you use them regularly. Be sure you check out any warehouse or buyer's club you join. If they aren't a significant player like these three warehouse clubs, you could be courting trouble because there are sketchy operators in this business. In general, you should not have to pay substantial upfront fees or be required to purchase a minimum amount to become a member.

I regularly shop at Sam's Club. This is not an endorsement over the other warehouse clubs. The reason I choose to buy there is that it is considerably closer to my house than its competitors. Gift cards are often available there at a considerable discount to the face value of the card. For example, I recently bought $50 gift cards to Boston Market and Prime Bar (a local *restaurant*, but they do have an impressive beer selection) for $40. We go to these restaurants regularly anyway, so I saved $20 on those two cards. Saving with gift card discounts by buying them for yourself only works if you were planning to spend money at the establishment anyway, and you don't lose the cards (it often happens to some people).

Another trick I have used to save money is buying gift cards around Christmas time to take advantage of discounts. Sometimes you can find discounts on gift cards at other times of the year. You can give the cards as a gift or keep them for yourself. Again, this only works if you were planning to buy the gift card as a gift or buy something at the business anyway.

Here are two examples. My family loves barbeque, and I do too. A southern barbeque chain that has restaurants near all of us offers a $5 bonus gift card for every $25 gift card bought in the month leading up to Christmas. I gift the $25 cards and keep the $5 cards, and everyone is happy. Yes, I tell my relatives proudly that I am getting a freebie by buying them a gift. They don't seem to mind. They do suggest that if I double my gift to them that I can double the amount of barbeque that I eat. Fortunately, I see the error in that logic from my point of view.

Another gift card I regularly buy around Christmas is a gift card to the hairstylist chain that I frequent. They charge $14 for a haircut for men. The gift card price per cut is only $10. In early December, I buy ten haircuts on the gift card (the number of cuts I get in a year), thus saving myself $40 over the next year. This past year I forgot to buy the gift card until the day after they last offered it. No gift card, bah! Over the next year, every time I had to pay $14, I cringed a little and berated myself internally. I cannot wait until Christmas so that I can go back to my frugal hair ways. Yes, frugal, not cheap. Cheap would be if I didn't tip, and I tip my stylist. My sister used to be a stylist, and if she found out I didn't tip, I would suffer terrible consequences. What consequences? That's the scary part; I don't know. The tipping will continue.

When buying furniture or large appliances or other expensive items, deal only with healthy, reputable businesses and pay with a credit card. If you pay with a credit card and the company goes bankrupt before you accept delivery, you can do a chargeback on your credit card. Therefore, you will not lose any money. If you pay by cash, check, or debit card and the company goes bankrupt, you will become a creditor just like everyone else the company owes. In other words, you will almost certainly lose all the money that you paid for the expensive item, and you will likely get nothing in return.

It is good to have hobbies, exercise interests, or other recreational pursuits. All work and no play make Jack and Jill dull kids. I didn't come up with this saying, but I did modernize it by gender neutralizing it, and it does make a good point. The whole reason for work should be so that we can enjoy life.

There are different levels of expenses in recreational pursuits. Some are very expensive, racing Lamborghinis. Some are quite reasonable, racing model cars. An old friend of mine used to collect toy trains. They looked cool, but there are very few hobbies that I would want to engage in less. Still, my friend thought it was a lot of fun. He went to toy train conventions and bought and sold trains. He only made enough money to pay for his expenses, but he enjoyed the trips. It was a great hobby for him. He garnered lots of joy, got to travel, and he essentially broke even moneywise.

A hobby that you enjoy that costs nothing is a great hobby. It is an excellent thought to keep in mind when deciding on recreational pursuits. What is this going to cost me and how much will I enjoy this pursuit.

Let's say you are trying to decide whether to take up tennis or golf. Both sports can be enjoyable and allow you to spend time with friends. But, at least financially speaking, tennis has excellent advantages. Tennis is much less expensive, generally takes less time, and offers more cardiovascular benefits. I have enjoyed both sports in the past, and I hope to enjoy them both in the future. But I enjoyed tennis a lot more in my poor youth, and I did not take up golf until I was almost forty. The reason was simple. Tennis costs less than golf.

If you have a strong desire to take up an expensive pursuit, Godspeed. If you are trying to decide between recreational pursuits that you may be engaged in for decades, you should consider the financial angle when deciding. If you find a hobby or recreational pursuit which can make you a little money, you have hit the jackpot. Still, please don't quit your day job too soon.

Keeping physically fit can help you to stay *fiscally* fit. If that didn't make you groan, you have an exceptionally high tolerance for bad puns. Congratulations, I think. Still, the statement is true. Keeping healthy lowers healthcare costs. Perhaps our government will eventually come up with a plan that reduces everyone's healthcare costs. Regardless, watching out for your health will probably save you money and will undoubtedly improve your life.

I have been a member of a fitness center for almost all the last three decades. Furthermore, I have used them extensively. I'd advise everyone to work out regularly, but you do not need a gym membership to do so. There are many ways to keep fit without the expense of health club memberships. You can walk, play tennis or basketball at a park, jog, do pushups, etc. I have found that having a gym membership helps me to keep motivated. But I have had plenty of friends that have kept fit without any regular monthly payments.

If you are a person that likes to work out at a gym, then the money spent on membership fees is money well-spent. Gym memberships, fitness trainers, and other workout program fees can become quite costly. I would never discourage anyone from spending their money on a fitness regimen that is working and that they enjoy. After all, there are few, if any, things more important than your health.

Still, it is not a good idea to spend wastefully in the pursuit of a healthy lifestyle. The fact that gym memberships and similar exercise expenses are substantial, recurring expenses makes them an important financial decision.

If you do decide to join a gym or employ a trainer or fitness expert, you should shop around and get recommendations from others just like you would for any other purchase. Fitness facilities and personal trainers often rival used car salespeople for high-pressure sales tactics.

If you are offered a contract for a fitness plan or facility, read it. Don't rely on what the salesperson said. If it is not in the contract, it does not matter what they promised you. You have a contract. Avoid signing a long-term contract. Most programs that offer these realize that most people will quit or not like their service, so you are likely not to like or use their service. This means you end up paying them for nothing. Pay the higher monthly fee until you know you want to continue using the service. Then, you can choose to sign up for long-term contracts that save you money. Even then, you need to make sure that there are opt-out clauses in case you must move, get injured, or have some other life-changing event that makes their service useless to you.

Fortunately, there are usually lots of fitness options available to most of us. That means that we can shop around. Competition is terrific for consumers, and it is great if you have fitness centers competing for your business. Don't forget to check the YMCA, YWCA, or local recreation centers and parks. They usually offer great deals if they meet your needs and are close to your location. The price of fitness services is important, but what is more important is the likelihood that you will use the service. I have discovered that you are much more likely to use a fitness center if it is close to your home or on your way to or from work. I once lived across the street from my gym. It was tough to come up with excuses not to work out. I don't think I have ever been in better shape than the time I lived there.

If you buy insurance, what are you purchasing? Insurance is paying someone else, an insurance company, to take a risk. Buying insurance makes sense if you are protecting yourself against a risk that you cannot comfortably afford to pay. Home, health, and auto insurance are types of insurance that cover potentially huge expenses that most of us are not willing to pay. Therefore, we purchase insurance for these risks.

Extended warranties are a type of insurance. With an extended warranty, you are paying someone else to take the risk that the item you are purchasing will breakdown. Thus, if the item malfunctions, the warranty provider will pay to fix the item, and you will not need to do so. Generally, purchasing an extended warranty for an item you can afford to replace if it fails is a colossal waste of money.

Therefore, I strongly advise against buying extended warranties unless the covered item breaking would present an extraordinary hardship on you and your finances. This means you should not purchase extended warranties for televisions, toasters, power tools, watches, or anything that costs under a few hundred dollars. Also, if your finances are in reasonably good shape, you should not buy extended warranties for items that cost up to a couple of thousand dollars.

The reason that companies push extended warranties so strongly is that they are almost sure that they will not have to pay out on the warranty. In other words, the item will not break. Please note that most extended warranties do not include coverage for accidents, owner negligence, or your dog chewing it up. In other words, most of the things that are likely to cause the item to quit working are not covered. Also, if you claim your warranty, you may end up having to spend time on paperwork, and spend time and frustration collecting on the warranty. Also, many warranties only cover parts and not labor. How convenient, the parts usually cost almost nothing, and the labor is the bulk of the cost.

Extended warranties have incredible margins for the retailer. A margin is the percentage of money that the retailer gets to keep from a sale. I used to work at one of the top ten retailers in the country. I was told that extended warranties had higher margins than any other item, by far. The margins on most extended warranties are around 80%. That's right. If you spend a dollar on an extended warranty, you will probably receive a benefit of 20 cents on average. It is hard to get rich getting a 20-cent return on a dollar invested. That is high-cost insurance. Again, avoid extended warranties unless the item breaking will result in an extreme financial hardship that you cannot cover.

Save on Housing, Transportation, and Your Child's Education

Purchasing a home can be the best investment you ever make. Conversely, buying a home can become a financial nightmare that mars your finances for years. Class dismissed!

Just kidding, I won't leave it at that. For most people, purchasing a home is a solid investment. A home purchase may have significant tax benefits because you may be able to deduct mortgage interest payments and other fees from your taxes. The tax benefits may disappear based on income levels, tax-filing status, and other factors. For example, the tax changes made under the Trump administration significantly raised the standard deduction and child tax credits. The tax changes resulted in lower taxes for many taxpayers. But it also resulted in a loss of the value of mortgage interest deductions.

Still, purchasing a home is not primarily an investment decision. It is mainly a lifestyle choice. I like renting because it allows me to move quickly, avoid maintenance issues, easily escape negative neighborhood changes, and invest any savings in high-return investments. On the other hand, my wife prefers the homeowner lifestyle. I love my wife and prefer to keep her happy, so I am and have been a happy homeowner for years.

Homeownership brings the pride of owning something important and customizing it to fit your needs. It also brings financial and time responsibilities. Typically, purchasing a home is an excellent way to build wealth and stability. On the other hand, if you buy a home without doing your homework and dealing with trusted representatives, it can become your most significant headache for years.

You should not buy a home unless you are reasonably sure that you want to live in that home for at least five years. The fees and stress involved in buying and selling a home make it inadvisable to buy a home with an expectation of living there for less than five years. It is okay to buy a home even though you are not 100% certain you will live there for five years. Otherwise, virtually no one would purchase a home. If it turns out that you want or have to move in less than five years, it will probably be fine, and you may even make a little money on your investment.

Once you decide to buy a home, you should get pre-approved for a mortgage and find the best real estate agent you can find. You will need to shop around for the mortgage and interview different real estate agents. You can choose to forgo hiring an agent, but I do not recommend this. The advice of a savvy agent is well worth the cost.

Your real estate agent and your mortgage representative will probably encourage you to buy the most expensive house that you can theoretically "afford." This amount will be related to the most costly mortgage you can attain. Coincidently (or not), the real estate agent and mortgage representative will make more money if you buy a more expensive house and borrow more. Hmm.

I highly recommend that you do _not_ buy the most expensive house you can afford. Buy the least expensive home that will best meet your needs and wants. A bigger home generally has more costly maintenance, taxes, and insurance. Also, money spent on a house is money that you cannot spend or invest elsewhere.

There are many other essential tips for buying a home. It is better to buy a house surrounding by more expensive homes than one surrounded by less expensive ones. Buy a home in a good school district. If you have or plan to have kids, a house with access to good public schools can save you hundreds of thousands of dollars of private school tuition. This is particularly important if you have kids, but also important if you do not have kids because it will still improve your resale value. Buying a home is such a significant investment that I highly recommend that you conduct extensive research into buying a home before you do so. Your research should include purchasing a good book on the subject.

Making just one mistake on a purchasing a home can be very costly. When I was looking for my first home, I made a significant error. While standing on the backyard deck of what would become my first home, I asked my real estate agent who owned the beautiful woods beyond my backyard. She replied that the homeowners' association owned the land. I purchased the house secure in the knowledge that there would be no development around my house that would negatively affect the value of my home. Wrong!

The homeowners' association did not own the land. The property developer did. After the subdivision was completed, the land was sold to a major grocery store chain. Eventually, that beautiful backyard view became a view of the *back* of a grocery store. That is right, dumpsters, employees on smoke breaks, and 18-wheelers unloading. Ah, beautiful nature. A few years later, I was finally able to sell it for 20% less than I would have been able to sell it for if I still had my forest view. Lesson learned.

I have done fine on every home I have owned since that first one because I now know to do my homework. I have bought one of the lower-cost homes in fully-developed neighborhoods in excellent school districts. My neighbors don't bring my property values down, they bring them up (I might hurt their property values, but I try not to).

Home mortgage interest may be tax-deductible. That is good, but the bad thing is that interest is still an expense. I have a 3.75% rate mortgage on my home. Depending on when you read this, that may seem incredibly low or ho-hum. Historically, 3.75% is a low rate, and it provided me a tax break in the first few years of my mortgage. My after-tax rate was around 3.00%. Since then, I no longer itemize my taxes because of changes in the tax code, and my after-tax rate has risen to 3.75%. I am in no hurry to pay off this mortgage because I prefer to invest any extra money I have in stock mutual funds. I am almost sure that this investment will earn well over 3.75% after taxes in the long-run.

If I had a significantly higher interest rate, say 7.00% or 8.00%, I would have a much higher interest in paying off my mortgage early. One way to think of paying your mortgage off first is that this is equivalent to earning the interest rate of your mortgage risk-free and tax-free. Therefore, if I had an 8.00% interest rate on my mortgage, I should pay this off early. Alternatively, I would have a challenging time earning 8.00% risk-free and tax-free on any other investment.

There are other risks and problems related to homeownership. Interest payments on a mortgage are tax-deductible for some people. Other expenses, such as maintenance, property taxes, and insurance, are not tax-deductible and tend to go up over time. Houses do not always go up in value. It is not uncommon to encounter underwater mortgages or lose money on home purchases. Therefore, buying a new house with an ever-increasing mortgage as you get progressively higher-paying jobs may be a terrific investment or a path to financial ruin.

Owning rental real estate offers tax advantages and can be a profitable business for knowledgeable and involved investors, but it is a business, not a passive investment. Income property can be a good investment if you know the market and enjoy managing it.

On the other hand, if you own a home, you are already heavily invested in real estate. Therefore, if you buy more real estate, your investments are less diversified. You may be putting too many of your eggs in one basket. Another drawback of owning a rental property versus other investments is that you won't get calls to fix a toilet or a roof on most other investments. You are likely to get this call if you own rental property, likely while you are on vacation or in some other enjoyable pursuit. Downer!

Purchasing shares in a real estate investment trust (REIT) is an excellent way to invest in real estate. These companies invest primarily in real estate, pay no corporate taxes, and must distribute most of their income to shareholders as dividends. Most generate reliable yearly income. Different REITs specialize in various types of real estate. For example, REITs may concentrate on medical, hotel, apartment, retail, storage, and warehouse properties. As with all investments, diversify your investment into more than a few REITs if you decide to take this route to real estate ownership.

Choosing where to live is an important financial decision. You'd be wise to put a lot of thought into this decision. For most of us, this is a selection that we must repeatedly make during our lifetime. I am confident that I have lived in over 25 different residences. I had to make a significant financial decision every time that I moved. Most people probably won't move as much as I have, but my experience is not an outlier. If you live in less than ten different locations during your adult life, you will have to make the residential choice fewer times than most Americans.

If you rent your residence, your rent will probably be your most significant expense. If you are buying your home, your mortgage payment will probably be one of your most significant expenses and investments. Yeah, this is an important financial decision.

Purchasing a home is a mediocre investment. Before the financial crisis of 2008, that statement would have been heresy. Homes were thought of as excellent, no lose investments. Now, we know that you can lose on a home investment and lose a lot.

Most information on resale values and the investment return on homes is provided by the home building and home lending industry. Any conflict of interest here? Yes. The information and news stories culled from industry-provided information tend to overstate the returns of owning a home. Frequently, the gains do not include the expenses of home-owning, such as taxes, insurance, maintenance, and sales commissions. Investments' returns look much more enticing if you ignore significant costs.

Also, many home valuation statistics ignore the fact that not all homes are the same. For example, let's say you see that the homes in your zip code have increased by 5% a year over the past ten years. That sounds great. You want to own. Unfortunately, this statistic probably ignores the fact that many of the homes in the area are new homes that are much bigger and more modern than most of the houses in the area. Newer, bigger, more modern homes sell for more. So, the average pre-existing home in the area may have had a value increase of much less than 5% a year.

On the other hand, owning a home has many advantages. There is something special about owning your own place. You can truly personalize your living space and benefit from any improvements that you choose to make to the property. Also, if you sell most things for more than you bought them, you usually must pay a capital gains tax. That is generally not true if you sell a home for a profit.

The most crucial financial determinant of whether you should buy or rent is the length of time you are planning to live in your residence. I advise you to rent your residence if you are not reasonably sure that you will live in it for more than five years. I make this recommendation because if you live in a home you are purchasing for less than five years, you will probably not do well financially on the transaction. The commissions, fees, taxes, and hassle associated with buying and selling a house within five years or less usually make it a poor investment financially.

I'd advise you never to buy a house to rent it out if you need to move later. It is complicated and often very costly to manage a rental property from afar. It can become a massive headache and make you lose sleep. Any investment that causes you to lose sleep is a bad investment.

If you choose to buy a house, you need to do extensive research. I'd suggest buying a good book. I purchased *110 Questions Every First-Time Home Buyer Should Ask: With Answers from Top Brokers from Around the Country* by Ilyce Glink before I bought my first home. I highly recommend it. The most recent edition I could find was from 2005, so you will also want to buy a more recent book on home buying. I suggest searching for "buying your first home" on Amazon or some other bookseller and purchasing a best-selling or highly rated book that seems to fit the bill. If you do not have the money or time to buy and read two books on purchasing a home, I suggest that you do not buy a home. The financial commitment is too big not to do your homework. I have heard dozens of stories about how great home purchases have improved finances. Conversely, I have heard dozens of stories about how buying a home has ruined someone's financial life. You want to be in the right group.

Although I want you to do your research before buying a home, I want to offer some basic tips. Your mortgage selection is an important financial decision that can go a long way towards making a satisfactory housing purchase. You should prequalify for a mortgage before you go house shopping. That way, you know how much you can afford to pay for a house and sellers will take you much more seriously than if you are not pre-approved.

Lenders will typically approve a loan value that is more than you want to spend. They don't care if you eat rice and beans for the next 30 years. You don't want to be house poor, living in a great place, but not able to afford life's little pleasures like going to the movies or eating out.

There are different rules of thumb to use to determine how much house you can afford. You should find some when you do your home-buying research. I will cover one called the *Rule of 43%*. Again, I caution you to be conservative. If you spend the maximum amount on a mortgage that you qualify for, the rest of your budget will be tight. You will probably encounter significant stress related to your finances.

To use the *Rule of 43%*, you first multiply your gross monthly income by 43%. Then you add up your monthly principal, interest, property taxes, and insurance (PITI) along with your utilities, car payment, student loans, and credit card payments to get your total monthly debt. If your total monthly debt is less than 43% of your monthly income, you can afford the mortgage.

Generally, you will have two decisions related to your loan: the length of the loan and whether you want a fixed-rate or adjustable-rate mortgage. The most common periods for fixed-rate loans are 15 and 30 years. With a 15-year loan, you will usually get a slightly lower interest rate, a significantly higher monthly payment, but you will pay off the mortgage much more quickly.

With an adjustable-rate loan, you will usually get a lower initial interest rate, sometimes much lower. This can be a very good thing, but be aware that the interest and your payment can go up a great deal over the life of the loan. The terms of adjustable-rate mortgages vary a great deal between different lenders. You must read the contract and know how your mortgage may adjust later.

Adjustable-rate mortgages can be a good choice but tread with caution. Adjustable-rate mortgages are likely a good option if you are not planning to stay in the home for more than five years or interest rates are high and likely to go down. If mortgage interest rates are low (less than 5% or 6%), I suggest a fixed-rate loan because it simplifies your financial situation and reduces mortgage payment risk.

If you are buying a home and paying a mortgage, you should regularly check (twice a year should do it) on home mortgage interest rates. If rates drop to around 2% less than your current mortgage interest rate, you should look into refinancing your mortgage. There will be no shortage of banks and other financial institutions willing to help you complete this process. Shop around for the best rate. Bankrate.com is an excellent place to start. Do not take money out of your home when you refinance. Refinancing reduces your equity and is a big step back in your overall savings.

The home buying process is rapidly changing due to technology. Many buyers and sellers even opt to forego hiring an agent. I recommend that first-time buyers employ a buyer's agent. A buyer's agent is legally obligated to represent the buyer, and they should give you valuable advice. Agent commissions are a significant expense, but a competent agent is more than worth it.

If possible, you should get buyer agent recommendations from friends. Also, online suggestions are worth a look. You should look for agents that have many listings and numerous sold homes in the location you are planning to locate. Finally, you should interview at least three agents. In general, part-time agents and agents just getting started will not do as good a job for you as experienced, successful full-time agents.

There are many other factors to consider when buying a home, too many to cover in this book. That is why you need to do your research. One of the most important factors I learned about in my research is to know your commute. If you are thinking about buying a home in a specific neighborhood, you should test the commute to and from that neighborhood during the time you usually commute to and from work.

The quality and time of a work commute is a significant determinant of quality of life. I had a one-hour commute each way (on a good day) with my least favorite house that I have owned. My ideal home had an eight-minute commute. I liked the one-hour house better than the eight-minute in almost every other way, but the commute differential outweighed all the other factors in determining which house I preferred.

In my experience, the importance of the work commute is underestimated by many home purchasers. They often underestimate the extra expense of transportation expenses for a longer commute because of higher gas and maintenance expenses and wear and tear on the car. Also, longer commutes significantly increase the possibility of being involved in an accident and the psychological and financial losses that accompany the accident. Also, a longer commute increases your chances of being late for dinner or missing important family events.

I found that doing a little math convinced me never again to have a one-hour commute like I had in my first house. The one-hour commute works out to two hours a day times five days a week, which equals 10 hours a week. Let's say you work 48 weeks a year (subtracting four weeks for vacation and holidays. That works out to 480 hours spent on the road per year. If you count that time on the road as part of your work as I do, that is the equivalent of working an additional twelve 40-hour workweeks a year. Twelve extra weeks of work? No, thank you.

There are many other essential tips that you need to know to increase your likelihood of making a good home purchase choice. Generally, you will do better financially if you buy one of the lowest-priced homes in a neighborhood as compared to one of the highest-priced. That way, you will be dragging down the value of your neighbors' homes instead of them dragging down the value of your home.

If you buy one of the last houses in a new subdivision, you can often get a better price. The sales office is a significant expense, and the builder(s) want to sell those last few houses quickly so that they can close the sales office sooner.

You can often get a good deal on one of the first houses in a new subdivision. Builders like to have people move in quickly so that the neighborhood starts to look like a neighborhood and not just a construction zone. There are two notable downsides to being one of the first people to move into a new community. Firstly, you will have to live with the annoyance of continuing construction, sometimes for years. Secondly, if the subdivision developer goes bust, you could end up living in an unfinished neighborhood. If this happens, the value of your home takes a major negative hit.

Once you own a home, if it goes up in value or you make years of payments, you may acquire home equity. You have home equity if your home is worth more than you owe on it. Home equity is a good thing. If you have home equity, this means that you will get some money if you sell the home. You should resist the urge to take a home equity loan. Home equity loans generally have a lower interest rate than most other loans. Interest on home equity loans is often tax-deductible, but they are risky loans to use. The reason is that if you cannot make your home equity loan payments, you may lose your home to the lender. That is a considerable risk. I'd advise you to build equity and forego the home equity loans.

The other half of making a home a sound financial decision is the decision to sell. When you sell your home, you must do your homework as well. Just like when buying a home, a good sales agent is usually more than worth their commission. Once you have found a reliable agent, take their advice on how to make your house saleable. It is a hassle to prepare a home for sale, but it is well worth the effort.

The first step to preparing your house for sale is to do maintenance, painting, and landscaping that needs to be done. You don't have to spend money unnecessarily. It is incredible what a little paint and a few annual plants can do. Simply removing ugly or broken items and keeping your home neat and clean will go a long way towards making it saleable. This can be surprisingly difficult to do, especially if you have kids, but it will go a long way towards selling your house quickly and for an acceptable price.

Your goal should be to make it look as if whoever lives in your house cleaned it right before they went on vacation. You want to remove all the clutter. This may mean that you need to rent a storage unit or better yet, you can get rid of things you are not using. A good rule of thumb is to sell or throw away anything that you have not used in the past year and are unlikely to use over the next year. Remove lower quality furniture and fixtures to make your home look better and roomier. Take clothes out of your closet that are out of season or that you are not planning to wear soon. It is amazing how spacious this trick will make your closets appear.

The most important thing you can do to increase your chances of selling your home is to clear out whenever someone is looking at your house. People will say they don't mind if you are there while they look, but it changes the way they look at the home. They will spend much less time looking, not feel comfortable discussing what they think of the house, and they will be thinking of it as your home and not as their potential home.

Have a plan for vacating the house at a moment's notice. Pick a local fast food joint and bring a book or your computer. If you have young kids, find a place they enjoy visiting. We sold our home when my kids were six and eight. They came to enjoy the calls to vacate the house when they realized it meant a visit to the local McDonalds with a kids' play space. They might even get an ice cream out of the deal.

A good roommate can be a beautiful thing. A bad roommate can be a terrible thing. Let me rephrase that, a bad roommate can be an awful, dreadful, unpleasant, horrendous, disastrous, terrible thing. I was once told that all good writers use a thesaurus, box checked. My use of the thesaurus is intended to emphasize that while roommates can greatly improve your financial situation and life in general, they can also make your life ghastly (I came up with that one on my own, no thesaurus needed).

There is no doubt that a good roommate can significantly improve your living situation. I have mostly had great roommates. That is no accident. I did my research, and I have never chosen a stranger as a roommate. The Army chose some roommates for me, but even there, I generally did okay because I am a pretty good roommate. That is a crucial component to getting good roommates; you must be a good roommate.

Let's start with the positives of having a roommate. Your rent, utilities, and many other living expenses are roughly cut in half. These are major expenses, and cutting them in half can have a major positive impact on your finances. There are many other benefits to having a good roommate. They provide added security, companionship, emergency help, transportation options, and social options. Also, if you are buying a home, don't forget that a good roommate can turn a good house investment into an excellent home investment. Let your roommate help you to build equity.

One of the best roommates I ever had was a work acquaintance that was not a particularly close friend of mine. I knew he was a friendly professional guy, but we had very different interests and personalities. We were both new to the city and our jobs, so we decided to take a shot at being roommates. It was a match made in Heaven.

We were both neat, quiet, and spent a lot of time outside our apartment. We both had steady jobs and had no problem paying the rent and other shared expenses. We could afford to buy our own food and would choose to share on occasion. We only saw each other a few hours a week, and that was usually spent having a pleasant little conversation or watching a television show together. He had nicer pictures, paintings, and furniture than I did, so he got to use his stuff, and I got to enjoy it for free.

For the most part, it was if I lived in my apartment alone but only paid half of the rent and utilities. Nirvana! There were other advantages. Occasionally, we would go to social events, and we could provide wingman duties to each other. Notably, I invited him to a singles event at a church I was considering attending, and we had a pretty good time. He had a better time than me. He met his future bride that day and continued attending the church while I moved on to a church that better suited my needs (where I met my wife ten years later). He got the better deal out of our roommate relationship, but we both benefitted.

I have had mostly good luck with being roommates with my friends and relatives, but that is because I have roomed with responsible friends and relatives. Also, I have done my part to make things work. Still, you should consider the fact that if you room with a friend or relative, and the roommate situation goes awry, your relationship can be permanently damaged. If you are considering a friend or relative as a potential roommate, be aware that any annoying habits they have will be magnified tenfold once you are roommates.

What about moving in with your significant other? I have some unconventional advice on this based on my experience and the experience of dozens of my friends. Firstly, living together is *not* like being married. It is very little like being married. Also, practically living together (often spending the night at each other's' place) is not the same as living together because of the impacts on finances and freedom. Living together is very easy to do and often relatively easy to undo. Marriage is a public legal, financial, emotional, and spiritual commitment. See the difference.

I am a religious person, and, like most religions, mine does not condone romantic couples living together without a marital commitment. Still, that is not the primary reason why I recommend living apart until you are married. The reason is simple. In my experience, when couples move in together without a marital commitment, it usually ends badly with significant emotional and often financial trauma. Of course, there are exceptions to this, but do you want to plan your life hoping that you are the exception.

Money is *not* everything. As a finance guy, it hurts me a little to write that, but the cliché is true. I would advise any couple contemplating cohabitating that includes saving money on their top three reasons for moving in together to keep their residences separate. If you are considering living together for a year or two before you decide to get married, don't do it. Suck it up and pay the extra rent for a little while. If you both have roommates, it may not even cost you anything extra.

Look at the decision from a financial point of view. If you are going to get married in two years, the extra years of paying more rent will have almost zero impact on your long-term finances. On the other hand, if you move in together before you are fully committed, you are much more likely to experience a breakup with painful psychological and financial costs.

For most of us, transportation is one of our most substantial expenses. Sometimes there are many options for transportation: buses, trains, cabs, Uber, Lyft, walking, biking, skateboards, pogo sticks, jet skis. You get the point. If you can use these lower-cost modes of transportation and they meet your needs, you should do so. Congratulations on good planning. Still, most of us need a car.

Cars are cool. They give us independence and flexibility. They also are expensive to buy, maintain, insure, and operate. Automobiles are a reoccurring expense. This increases the importance of keeping automobile expenses under control. Making one lousy decision about costs is not good. Making the wrong decision about an expense that is going to reoccur for months or years is much worse.

If you need to buy a car, purchase one that meets your needs at a reasonable price. Don't pay up to get an impressive looking car or because it is so cool. It is okay to purchase a car just because it is sexy or hip once you have made your fortune. Before that, think of practicality and safety. In general, bigger cars are safer. It is simple physics. You may find small cars rated highly for safety, but they are usually highly rated in comparison to other small cars. Once again, it is simple physics. When a big, heavy car hits a small, lightweight vehicle, the occupants of the bigger car typically fare better than the smaller car's occupants. Also, a bigger car generally fares better when hitting a stationary object such as a tree or telephone pole. Bigger cars typically cost more than small cars, so there is a trade-off between safety and finances. I prefer to buy the safest car possible within a reasonable budget.

The easiest way to improve safety is to drive safely and avoid unnecessary trips in the car. Driving less will also save money on gas, maintenance, insurance, and other expenses. Other ways to improve safety include keeping your car well-maintained and consider taking defensive driving classes. Develop good driving habits, braking, and accelerating slowly saves money on maintenance and gas, and it improves safety.

When calculating the cost of your auto, calculate the total cost of ownership, including maintenance, gas, and insurance. Don't skimp on required maintenance because it will probably cost you more in the long run. Car maintenance establishments often recommend more maintenance than is necessary because getting paid is good. I use the Carfax® app to track the maintenance of my family's vehicles. I am sure there are other useful apps out there, but I have chosen this one. It is advantageous to pull up my vehicle records on my phone and inform a mechanic that my car does not need another injector cleaning.

Purchasing a car is a significant financial decision, and you need a good process to do it well. I advise buying a nearly new used car with relatively low mileage if you can afford it. You can save thousands of dollars and get a vehicle that is still under warranty.

I have bought my last few cars at CarMax®. I love their no-haggle pricing and service. AutoNation USA and Driver's Mart also offer no-haggle pricing. Can you get a better deal by shopping on your outside of a dealership? Maybe, if you are quite knowledgeable. If so, go for it. It is not worth it to me.

I like that CarMax® lets you return the car within a few days and offers a 90-day warranty on their used cars. I also love the fact that they try hard to sell extended warranties. That tells me that they have inspected the vehicle, and they don't think anything is wrong with it. After all, it would be foolish of them to push extended warranties if they thought the car was going to have problems during the warranty period. I don't take the warranty but take them if you must.

If you have a car you want to trade-in, it has been my experience that CarMax® will give you an excellent price for your trade-in. The last three times that I have had a car to trade-in, CarMax® has offered me roughly double what other dealers have provided me. They will give you a price in writing that they are willing to pay for your car and give you three days to try and find someone else that will offer you more for the vehicle. I haven't seen any that have come close. There is nothing to lose by having CarMax® evaluate your car other than a little time.

One of the best things about the CarMax® offer for your trade-in is that the offer stands whether you buy a car from CarMax® or not. That's great. If you choose to go to a traditional dealer, make sure you do your research on prices before visiting the dealer using a research service such as TrueCar (truecar.com) or Edmunds (edmunds.com). You should always keep your trade-in value negotiation, new car price negotiation, and loan rate negotiation separate. Most dealers will try to tie these negotiations together to try and confuse you and take advantage of you. If you allow them to lump these negotiations together, you will not know what you are paying for the car, or receiving for your trade-in, or what interest rate you are truly paying for the loan.

You should get pre-qualified for a car loan from your credit union or bank. They will give you an interest rate quote. If the dealer can beat this rate, you can let them finance your purchase. If not, stick with your pre-qualified lender. Also, ask the dealer to give you the trade-in value that they are willing to pay even if you do not buy from them. It probably won't be anywhere near what CarMax® will pay. After that, you can negotiate any purchase price without clouding the decision with other factors. It is straightforward; a lower price is a better price.

When you go into a dealer, you will probably be asked, "How much are you looking to pay each month?" Don't answer that question unless you say, "as little as possible." They probably won't laugh, but that is the correct answer.

You should decide what type of car you need and try to get it for as low a price as possible. You should *not* buy the best car you can afford (or barely or almost afford). Purchasing an extended warranty for a vehicle is rarely a good idea. Leasing a car instead of buying for a business might make sense. Leasing a car might make sense if you are planning to buy a new car every two or three years, but don't do this unless you are already rich.

Automobile insurance is a significant reoccurring expense. Mine is well over $1,000 a year, and my wife and I have excellent driving records. Yours could be much higher. Therefore, you want to shop around extensively. My wife and I have used GEICO for decades, and they have provided us excellent service. I shop around every five years or so, and I have not found another insurer that will come close to meeting their price. Still, the insurance market is very different for different people. GEICO may not provide as good a deal for younger drivers or drivers with a poor driving record. You should shop around when purchasing car insurance and continue to explore other insurers rates as time goes on. You can usually save money by accepting a higher deductible on your coverage. Be sure to ask about that. Automobile insurance is expensive enough to make it worth your time to try to get the best rate possible.

If you need to rent a car while traveling, you will find that the rates vary a great deal by the provider and the type of vehicle you are renting. You can save by shopping around. Most people can avoid the need to purchase rental car insurance if their credit card or auto insurance covers rental cars. You must check to make sure you are covered. You can also save a considerable amount of money by choosing to return the vehicle with a full tank of gas that you pump yourself. Be sure you don't forget to fill the car up before returning it, or you will usually get hit with a significant charge.

Giving substantial amounts of money to children is a hassle. If you only provide a child a few hundred dollars a year, I wouldn't argue against merely giving it to them. You should check to make sure you are not violating tax laws. I would never recommend violating any laws, but tax collectors generally don't put a lot of effort into collecting small disputable amounts.

The Uniform Gifts to Minors Act (UGMA) takes effect if you give substantial gifts to minor children. It can get complicated. Therefore, I advise you to hire a financial advisor or conduct rigorous research on the tax implications before you give thousands of dollars to a minor.

You should start saving for your children's education at a very early age. If you want to give money to a child that will help them to get an advanced education beyond high school, a 529 plan is the way to go. As you may gather from the catchy name, 529 plans were established by the federal government to provide a tax-efficient means for parents, grandparents, or even friends to contribute to college savings for children. They are an excellent way to help a child save for college. These plans have some significant advantages to saving money for college outside a 529 plan.

As of 2018, You can contribute up to $15,000 a year to a 529 plan. You can contribute over $200,000 in total to a 529 plan; the exact amount varies by state. These values are for each contributor to each child's plan. So, for example, if a married couple wanted to contribute to three separate grandchildren's plans in any given year, they could provide $15,000 from each grandparent to each child. This would be $30,000 for each of the three children for a total of $90,000.

Most states have 529 plans, and the quality of plans vary significantly from state to state. Some programs have low investment fees, and some have fees and annual expenses that are quite high. In some cases, if you use the 529 plan from the state in which you reside, you may get tax breaks.

Using a 529 plan has several advantages over merely giving money to children. Contributions to a 529 plan are not deductible, but earnings grow federal tax-free, and withdrawals taken out to pay for college are not taxed. The donor controls the account, so if the child decides to forgo college and search for unicorns and Sasquatch, they cannot merely take the money. In this situation, the donor can direct the funds to another beneficiary or even take the money for themselves. Note that any money that is taken out for non-educational purposes will be taxed and have a 10% penalty.

Most states have 529 plans, but many have lousy, costly plans. I have been using the Utah plan (uesp.org) for my children for over a decade, and I plan to use it until they graduate. I have never lived in Utah, and you do not have to live in a state to use its plan. I chose the Utah state plan for my children because it had low fees and annual costs associated with its Vanguard funds. I can recommend the Utah 529 plan as one of the best available. If you do some research, you may be able to find a plan that better suits your needs.

You have several different investment options in most plans. Remember that stock funds tend to have higher and more volatile long-term returns than other funds. Also, funds with lower annual costs tend to outperform similar funds over the long-term. Some states offer tax advantages to state residents to use their plan, so you may be able to find a program that is preferable to the Utah plan. In any case, the Utah plan is a solid value.

Choosing the state plan you will use for your 529 plan is a crucial decision, and beyond the scope of this book. Here are the websites I used to research 529 plans:

savingforcollege.com
investopedia.com/terms/1/529plan.asp
sec.gov/reportspubs/investor-publications/investorpubsintro529htm.html

Speaking of college, planning, and paying for the education of children is one of the most significant expenses involved in raising kids. Those expenses can be significantly reduced through proper planning, responsible saving, and reasonable goals.

Do not use retirement savings to pay for a child's education. This is robbing Peter to pay Paul. If you can avoid it, you do not want to be a burden to your children.

Start planning and saving from the time your children are born or even before that. If you are planning to buy a house, it is a great idea to know the quality of the local public schools. If you can send your kids to a high-quality public school instead of a private school, you can save tens of thousands of dollars for over ten years. Even if you do not have children, a house that is zoned for high-quality public schools adds a lot to the value of your home when you resell.

In many states, the education environment for children is rapidly changing. Charter schools and school choice programs are growing. School zones often change quickly, especially in developing, thriving neighborhoods. Therefore, if you wish to ensure that your toddler is zoned for a specific high school, you should buy a house very close to that high school. Also, you should realize that the high school might not be so great when your child is old enough to attend it. The bottom line is that public school quality dramatically affects the value of homes, but future public-school quality is not entirely predictable. Still, you should incorporate local public-school quality into your home purchase decision. Public schools have a tremendous impact on your home investment and the cost of a quality education for your children.

Paying for education, either yours or your child's, is usually a significant expense. The cost of a quality education can vary greatly. Frequently, an education at a state school can cost very little or may even be free. It is important to note that money borrowed for an education has to be repaid (even if you do not graduate). This may change because many politicians are advocating for the forgiveness of student loans, but future political actions are quite unpredictable. If you can comfortably afford an education at an ivy-covered private school, have fun. If not, try to get the most value for your investment.

I want to take a moment to state that four-year colleges are not for everyone. If you have a child that is not a particularly good student or has no desire to spend another four years in school, that's okay. They will probably need a little more education or an apprenticeship program to have a successful career. But there are plenty of solid careers that do not require a four-year degree. This is especially true if your child has a passion for a potentially lucrative career. Numerous careers are in high demand, yet don't require a bachelor's degree. I am always on the lookout for a quality mechanic, electrician, or plumber. I also know from experience that the hourly rate for these positions is pretty good.

If your child does choose to pursue a four-year degree, you will soon find out that the cost of college ranges from costly to crazy-expensive. State schools (especially in your state) tend to be much less expensive than private schools. The financial aid that your child can get for attending various schools can vary wildly. This is especially true if your child is an excellent student, has an exceptional talent, or is an accomplished athlete. The distance of the school from your home can affect total college costs a great deal. This is especially true if your child wants to visit home often or you want to visit them. Living costs also differ a great deal depending on the location of the school.

Selecting a college should be a joint decision between the parents and the child. An essential step to choosing a college is to calculate the full cost of attending a potential candidate after factoring in financial aid. Grants and scholarships (money you do not have to pay back) are a very different form of financial assistance from loans (money you must pay back). Many people mix these two under a big umbrella of financial aid. That is a major mistake.

I have told my daughters repeatedly that my number one goal for them as it pertains to college is for them to graduate without debt. They are only in their teens, but they already respond with a little exasperation and complete accuracy when I ask them what's my college goal for them. I am doing my job.

If your children go to college, one of your primary goals should be for them to graduate with minimal debt. One key to accomplishing this is to encourage your child to not fall in love with a school. It is much better if the school falls in love with your kid by offering them scholarships, special living accommodations, or employment opportunities. It happens.

But wait, haven't we been told that it is best to attend the highest-ranked, most elite college that accepts our children? Yes, we have been told this, primarily by representatives of the elite universities. There is a lot of evidence that this is not sound advice though.

The primary reason that graduates of elite universities succeed is that these universities only accept elite high school students. Research suggests that elite high school students that attend other less prestigious (and usually much less expensive) universities succeed at the same level. So, good students succeed if they attend respectable schools, and they graduate with a lot less debt. Currently, my teenage children are excelling in school. When the time comes to pick a school, I would prefer my children to choose a quality state school and graduate with no debt. I much prefer this to them graduating from an Ivy League school with $200,000 in debt.

Firstly, the most crucial factor in school choice is to attend one that that you are highly likely to complete your education. Matriculating for two or three years of college and then dropping out is costly and provides little advantage in the job market. In fact, many people see this as a sign of someone that does not finish the job. Working at a coffee shop while you pay off your student loans is not a great way to start a career.

I believe the second most important college decision is the choice of a major. This is admittedly difficult for most students. An ideal major is one that the student has a great passion for and one that has excellent chances of employment at a high starting rate of pay with exceptional opportunities for advancement. That's a lot to ask.

If your child has a passion for such a major, you are truly blessed. If like most of us, your child either has no real career passion or a passion for a field in which they are unlikely to find employment, there will have to be trade-offs. It is a difficult decision, but the main goal should be to get that degree. It is preferable to major in a subject that will allow you to start a career that you are passionate about and that you end up working in successfully for the rest of your life. Still, choosing the wrong major is not a life sentence. In our modern economy, most professionals change careers, often more than once. I know I have done so. Sometimes, it involves a step back career-wise, but it can be worth it if you make the change to pursue your passion. I know I am pleased that I made the career changes that I made.

So, to summarize, the goal of going to college should be to graduate with a major that will lead to a satisfying career with as little debt as possible. It can be accomplished, so start planning for success in this vital area as early as possible.

Chapter 5: Investment Fundamentals

First: Save for a Rainy Day

Once you are making enough money to more than cover your living expenses, it is time to start making investments. Sound investments are a beautiful thing. It is great to earn money through hard work. It is incredible to invest money to make more money without any additional effort.

Earlier I stated that your first savings goal should be to have 3 to 6 months' worth of living expenses in emergency savings. For your short-term savings and emergency funds, it is best to find the savings account, CD, or money market fund that pays the highest rate of interest. Importantly, many money market funds and some CDs are not federally insured by the FDIC. That is probably okay, especially if the money market fund is run by a large, well-known, respectable company like Vanguard, Charles Schwab, or Fidelity.

We use a savings account at our local bank and a Vanguard Federal Money Market Fund. The funds at the bank are readily accessible, and the Vanguard funds are available with a slight delay, but the Vanguard account earns a decent interest rate for short-term funds. The main thing is the funds should be safe and convenient but shop around using Bankrate.com and other sources to get the best return.

As you become more financially secure, you may choose to reduce your funds in emergency accounts to only one or two months of expenses. We have moved most of our emergency funds into a low-cost high-dividend stock fund from Vanguard. This is not a good idea for someone with little short-term and long-term savings. But we feel comfortable with the risk that we may have to liquidate this investment in an unfavorable environment (low stock prices) to pay emergency expenses. The extra income we get from this investment and its rise in value through the years have made this a lucrative if unconventional, form of emergency savings.

Interest rates, stock market returns, and inflation are notoriously tricky things to predict both in the short-term and long-term. Therefore, only short-term US-government insured investments are virtually free of risk. Unfortunately, these safe short-term investments have lower average returns than longer-term riskier investments in the long run.

Most people are risk-averse. This means that they will not invest in something with risk unless they are compensated with a higher average rate of return on their investment. This is rational behavior. It becomes irrational when a person avoids risk at all costs on all of their investments, thus guaranteeing terrible near-zero returns on all of their investments. Therefore, avoiding all risks ensures awful long-term investment returns.

The sooner that one needs the money from an investment, the safer the investment should be. Savings accounts, bank certificate of deposits (CDs), and money market funds are good options if you have an investment window of fewer than three years. If you do not need the funds from an investment in the next five years, stock and bond mutual funds become a better option because of their superior record of long-term returns.

If you have funds to invest in a long-term taxable account, an investment in stocks that don't pay dividends or a stock mutual fund that holds low-dividend stocks provides income tax advantages. You will not need to pay taxes on any gain in the value of your investment until you decide to sell the investment. Any dividends you receive will be taxed, but these will be low by design.

I started investing in my twenties. Most sound investments make money in most years. Few investments make money *every* year. Even great investments usually lose money in some years.

Still, if you invest wisely, the likelihood of you making money (and lots of it) over the long-term is exceptionally high. I started investing in my twenties, and I have made somewhere around an 8% to 10% over the last thirty years. That is not because I am a genius investor. That is just the average return of owning stocks over the long-term.

The subject of making wise investments is discussed in greater detail elsewhere in this book. You should understand that investing your money wisely is a key component of not being poor and a crucial element to getting rich slowly.

My preferred method of investment is to invest in the stocks of stable, profitable companies. My approach is a method that has made countless people wealthy over the last century or two. Still, many individuals may have other investment options.

Stocks, Bonds, and Mutual Funds

The two most common long-term investment securities are stocks and bonds. Even though most people have heard the terms "stocks" and "bonds" quite often, most people don't know precisely what they are. It is impossible to understand a good retirement savings plan without understanding the basics of stocks and bonds.

Let's start with an explanation of bonds. Simply put, if you invest in a bond, you are lending a company or government money. In return, the company or government will pay you interest until the bond matures, and then they will pay you the original loan (or principal) amount back.

Major bond categories include corporate bonds issued by a corporation, municipal bonds issued by a local or state government or government agency, and U.S. Treasuries issued by the federal government.

Taxes must be paid on income from corporate bonds. Interest from municipal (often called muni) bonds are exempt from federal taxes and usually from state and local taxes in the state that issues them. U.S Treasury bonds interest incur federal taxes but are exempt from state and local taxes. If you buy a bond for a price that is lower than you sell it for later, this is a capital gain, and it is taxed for all types of bonds. Similarly, if you by a bond for a price less than the original principal amount and receive the principal back at maturity, you owe taxes on the gain.

U.S. Treasuries are considered risk-free in that you are guaranteed to get all interest payments and principal back at maturity. The federal government can create new money, so there is virtually no chance that you will not be paid, barring a zombie apocalypse or similar calamity.

Most municipal and corporate bonds are reasonably low risk, meaning that you are highly likely to receive all of your interest payments and have your principal returned. But these bonds have risk. They are not as safe as treasuries or FDIC savings accounts.

Even U.S. Treasuries have some risk, namely interest rate risk. Let's say you buy a 30-year Treasury bond that pays a 3% interest rate when inflation is running at 1%. Initially, you are getting a positive real rate of return (your return above the inflation rate). If over time, inflation rises to 5%, your return is now not keeping up with inflation. That is not good.

You might think that in this scenario, you can sell the Treasury bond to someone else. Unfortunately, the problem is that as inflation rises, market interest rates rise, and the price of bonds fall. Therefore, you would have to take a loss on your bond if you sold it after inflation has already risen. This scenario applies to all bonds, as interest rates rise, bond prices fall.

In general, the higher the interest rate on a bond, the higher the risk. Bonds that have a considerable amount of risk are called speculative (or junk) bonds. This means you may not get your money back. Ouch! If you decide to invest in bonds, don't merely go for bonds with the highest interest rate. The higher return comes with a cost of higher risk.

Most bonds are rated by one of the three main credit rating agencies (Fitch, Standard & Poor's, and Moody's) based on their risk. These ratings are generally broken down into ten classes and two major categories, speculative and investment grade. No one should ever invest in speculative (high-risk) bonds unless they are an expert in bonds.

We have covered bonds in broad categories and characteristics here, but there is a myriad of different types of bonds and features. Each bond is an individual contract, like any loan contract, and there can be any number of legal complexities. For example, some bonds which are called convertible bonds can be converted into stock under specific conditions.

Oy, what to do? Fortunately, if you want to invest in bonds, you do not have to invest in individual bonds. I recommend that you do not invest in individual bonds. Also, I practice what I preach. I have never invested in an individual bond and I don't plan ever to do so. There is a safer way to invest in bonds that does not take a great deal of expertise, and that is to invest in a bond mutual fund. We discuss how to do that in a separate section of the book.

Stocks are often mentioned along with bonds, but the two are very different. If you buy a bond, you are lending money to a company or a government. If you buy a share of common stock, you become a part-owner of a company. That doesn't mean that you have much control or power over the company. Shareholders generally have almost no influence over the management of a company in which they own shares.

For example, let's say you bought 100 shares of Disney at $100 in 2018 for $10,000. An investment that size should give you some juice, right? Maybe you should give the CEO a call and tell him about some changes that should be made at Disney World. Nope! It turns out that at the time, Disney had 1.5 *billion* shares outstanding. This means that your 100 shares represent ownership of 0.000007% of the company. You are definitely a minority shareholder.

Don't despair. Your ownership entitles you to a share of the company's profits. Sometimes those profits are paid out as dividends. This means money is deposited into an account of your choosing. The account might be a retirement account, a savings account, or a checking account.

Any profits not paid out as dividends are reinvested in the company, which should raise the value of your shares over time. Eventually, most people sell their shares. The stock of most companies rises over time, especially if they are profitable companies. Therefore, if everything works out as expected and hoped for, you will eventually sell your shares for considerably more than you purchased them.

You made money. This is how things should work, although losing money in stocks over the short-term is relatively common. Fortunately, stocks usually go up over time. After all, if you invest money in ownership of a profitable company, wait a few years, and then sell your stake, you should make money. Capitalism rocks!

Of course, if you make money, you will almost always have to pay taxes on these gains. You will be taxed on dividends and capital gains (the amount that your proceeds from the sale of your stock exceeded your purchase price). The good thing about paying capital gains and dividend taxes is that you only pay them when you make money.

Most people should not invest in individual stocks. It is better to invest in stock mutual funds unless you are an expert in stocks. Many financial experts argue that even stock experts are better off investing in stock mutual funds. I will explain why in later sections. The good news is that you can benefit from owning stocks without knowing much about stocks at all.

Still, I think it is a good idea to have a basic understanding of what stocks are and some of their characteristics. The important thing to keep in mind is that that ownership of a share of stock represents partial ownership of a company. Therefore, investing in stocks is not gambling, as many have suggested in the past. Investing in stocks is investing in a business. If you invest in reliable companies, you are highly likely to make money over time. For example, if you purchase shares in Microsoft, Exxon, Walmart, McDonalds, and Proctor & Gamble for twenty years, you are highly likely to make money on these investments.

In general, you should not invest a significant amount of money in your own company's stock. That is, unless they give you the shares as part of your compensation, or you can buy it at a sizable discount. The reasoning is simple. If the company has problems, you may end up out of a job. If this happens, the stock of the company generally goes down. Therefore, if the company has problems, you do not want to lose your job at the same time as one of your most significant investments goes down in value.

There is one prominent example of when it may be a good idea for anyone to invest in an individual stock. If your company offers the opportunity to purchase the company's shares at a discount, this may be too good of a deal to turn down. For example, I worked for a company that allowed employees to buy stock at a 15% discount to the market price with the requirement that the stock had to be held for at least one year. I purchased all of the stock I was allowed to buy and sold it a year later.

I didn't sell the stock because I thought It was a bad investment. I sold it because I did not want to have too much money invested in just one company. This was true, no matter what I thought of the investment. This strategy allowed me to make a market return plus 15%. Therefore, if the stock price didn't move at all, I still made a 15% return on my investment. If the stock went up 10%, I made 25%. As long as the stock did not fall more than 15% during the year, I made money. That is an investment that is too good to turn down.

Specific stock information can get complicated rather quickly. That is one of the reasons that it is not a good idea to invest in individual stocks unless you are an expert. Some major categories of stocks you may hear about include value stocks and growth stocks, and small, large, and mid-cap stocks.

Value stocks are stocks that appear to be trading for a bargain price. In general, the revenues and earnings of value stocks are growing slowly or even contracting. Therefore, an investor can usually buy shares of the stock for a low price relative to current revenues and profits. Growth stocks are stocks that have revenue and earnings that are growing rapidly.

The market capitalization, often called market cap, of a company, indicates the overall value of the company. A company's market capitalization is found by multiplying the number of shares of a company by the share price. Companies with larger market capitalizations tend to have higher revenue and earnings. In short, large market cap companies are larger than mid-cap companies, which are larger than small-cap companies.

Historically, value stocks have earned a higher return for investors over the long-term. Also, small-cap stocks have tended to earn a higher return than mid-cap stocks, which have earned a higher return than large-cap companies. Of course, there is no guarantee that these patterns will hold in the future. In my opinion (and those of many people smarter than me), these patterns will likely continue. Still, even if I am right, it may take years for these patterns to hold. As I write this, the long-term trends have not held for the last few years as large-cap and growth stocks have outperformed small-cap and value stocks.

Preferred stock is a special type of stock. Preferred stock is very different than common stock. Common stock, which is, well, more common, represents actual ownership in a company. Preferred stock is unique and does not represent actual ownership. It is often advantageous for one corporation to own another corporation's preferred stock because of tax advantages. In general, individuals should not own preferred stock because individuals gain no tax advantage by owning preferred stock. There are rare exceptions, but they are too limited to consider here. I have never owned preferred stock, and I doubt I ever will. I suggest you do the same.

There are other specialized types of investments that trade on the stock exchange, some of which are not stocks. Master Limited Partnerships (MLPs) trade like stocks, and they can be reasonably good investments with tax advantages that represent ownership of a company. Still, they are complicated and should be avoided unless you make yourself extremely knowledgeable about their nature.

Real Estate Investment Trusts (REIT) are stocks that entail ownership of a firm that invests primarily in real estate. REITs have certain tax advantages, and they can be excellent investments that generate significant dividend income. Still, caution is recommended when investing in individual REITs. Much like investing in a home, you want to know what you are investing in before you write the check.

Exchange-Traded Funds (ETF) and closed-end funds also trade on stock exchanges. They appear to be similar to individual stocks, but they are much closer to a stock mutual fund. Most ETFs and closed-end funds represent ownership in the stocks or bonds of numerous companies. ETFs and closed-end funds are *usually* useful investments. Still, only knowledgeable investors should invest in them.

Investing in individual stocks is not necessary or recommended for most people. Investing in stock mutual funds is recommended. There are two primary reasons for this. First, stock and stock mutual fund ownership, both of which represent ownership in corporations, have been lucrative investments over the long-term. This is highly likely to be true in the future. Secondly, specialized expertise is required to be a superior stock investor, but no specialized knowledge is needed to be an exceptional investor in stock mutual funds.

Investing in individual stocks can be tempting, especially if you hear of others making fortunes by timing the market or day trading. Market timing sounds sensible, buy stocks when their prices are low and sell them when their prices are high. It would be a great idea if it were that easy. The problem is that most people will buy stocks when they think prices are low, but prices may go lower. A more common mistake is selling stocks when they think prices are high, but stocks keep going higher and never look back.

Research shows that market timers tend to panic and sell when stocks are low and get caught up in euphoria and buy when stocks are high. Selling low and buying high is not a good strategy, but that is what many market timers end up doing.

Market timers can spend a lot of time not invested in stocks earning little or no returns while the stock market soars. I would market time if I thought I could be successful at it, but I do not. Most experts recommend buying stocks and holding for the long-term. That is my investment philosophy and what I recommend.

Day trading is more dangerous and can result in great wealth destruction. Day trading is the practice of buying a stock and selling it for a small gain in a few hours or few days. This method can be effective when the stock market is rising overall. It can be disastrous if the stock market is going down. Another disadvantage of day trading is that any short-term profits you make will usually be taxed at a higher rate than long-term gains or dividends. Also, you will incur more transaction fees and losses due to bid-ask spreads. Bid-ask spreads refer to the fact that individual investors pay a higher price (ask price) to buy a stock than they receive (bid price) to sell a stock.

If you become interested in investing, you will probably have friends that make money using market timing and day trading. You will almost certainly incur commercials encouraging you to engage in market timing and day trading to get rich quick. People have succeeded in using these methods. Those with these extraordinary success stories tend to tell their friends and end up on commercials. The countless people that have lost most of their life savings using these strategies rarely tell their friends and never end up on commercials. I strongly urge you to resist the temptation to day trade or engage in market timing.

Picking the best stocks or bonds to buy is an extremely complicated job for those that are not experts. I do not recommend that most people even try. The good news is that you do not have to pick your stocks or bonds. Evidence indicates that most people are better off if they do not.

There is a better alternative called a mutual fund. Mutual funds pool funds from many investors to invest in a diversified portfolio of stocks or bonds and sometimes other assets. Larger mutual funds have thousands of investors. The three most common forms of mutual funds are common stock, bond, and balanced mutual funds.

Balanced funds invest in both stocks and bonds, usually in a fixed percentage such as 60% stocks and 40% bonds. Over the long term, a balanced fund is likely to garner lower returns than a stock fund, but with much less volatility. Balanced funds make sense for people that want good long-term returns with fewer years that have negative returns. My favorite balanced fund is Vanguard's STAR fund. This fund offers exposure to stocks and bonds from around the world. It is exceptionally well-diversified and has low annual expenses.

Mutual funds from reputable providers are safe. They are heavily regulated and provide a myriad of information about what they invest in and their past returns.

Here comes some excellent news. If you invest in a particular type of mutual fund, you will almost certainly do better than the average investor. Even better, you will almost certainly do better than investors that use expensive experts with fancy MBAs from the best schools.

This type of mutual fund is a low-cost, no-load index fund. Index funds buy the stocks or bonds that are part of an index such as the S&P 500. There is some controversy over whether index bond funds have had better returns than actively managed funds in the long-term. Therefore, if you choose to invest in a bond mutual fund, you should look for low annual fees and good past returns.

There is minimal controversy over whether stock index funds have done better than actively managed stock funds in the past. Over the long-term, index stocks have solidly outperformed actively managed funds. Furthermore, it is highly probable that index funds will outperform in the future. There are a few reasons why.

First, index funds generally incur significantly lower annual management and "12b-1" marketing fees than actively managed funds. These annual fees must be reported as an expense ratio. These reported fees are the percentage of funds invested that are spent annually on administrative, management, and other fees.

For example, as of April 2018, the Vanguard 500 Index Fund (which invests in S&P 500 stocks) had an expense ratio of 0.14%. This means that if you invested $3,000 in this fund, they would charge you $4.20 in annual fees for managing your investment and providing you statements and tax information. This is a very low fee policy. For comparison, it is not unusual for stock mutual funds to have an expense ratio of 1.00% or 2.00% or even more per year. This may not sound like a huge difference, but in our example, your annual fees would go up to $30 at 1.00% and $60 at 2.00%.

These higher fees can dramatically eat into your annual returns. This is especially true once you consider that you have to pay these fees year after year. Over ten year, the fees would be $42 (0.14%), $300 (1.00%), and $600 (2.00%). This is only if your investment didn't grow past $3,000. In all probability, your investment should grow quite a bit over ten years. If this happened, the difference in fees paid would grow even more.

A second reason that low-fee index funds almost always outperform actively managed funds is that index funds, by definition, earn returns that are very close to the index average. Index funds generally earn returns that are slightly below the index average because the small annual fees do hinder performance a little.

On the other hand, actively managed funds often perform significantly above or below the average. Still, if you take the average return of all the actively managed funds, their returns will be very close to the index return. On average, actively managed funds have returns that equal the index (before fees). But their fees are almost always higher than index funds. So, after expenses, most actively managed funds have sub-par returns. Very few mutual funds beat the market index consistently because it is challenging to perform above average by an amount higher than the fees year after year. For example, a fund with a 2% expense ratio would have to outperform the market by 2% a year to be a good investment. It turns out that this is a Herculean feat that few mutual fund advisors are capable of attaining.

If your mutual fund is held in a taxable account, index funds have another significant advantage over actively managed funds. Index funds are almost always more tax-efficient than actively managed funds. If you own either type of fund, you will have to pay taxes on any dividends the funds generate. But actively managed funds tend to buy and sell stocks much more often than index funds. If the fund sells a stock for a higher price than it was purchased, mutual fund shareholders will have to pay a tax on this capital gain. This is true even if you do not choose to sell any of your mutual fund holdings.

Hopefully, I have you convinced that a low-fee stock index mutual fund is your best bet for investing in stocks. But I mentioned "low-cost, no-load index fund" earlier. "Fee" and "cost" are synonymous, but what does "no-load" mean. A "load" is a fee that is charged to the investor when the fund is bought (a front-end load) or sold (a back-end load).

For example, let's say a fund has a 5% front-end load. This means you will lose 5% of your investment immediately upon investing in the fund. If you invest $1,000, you pay a $500 load, and only $950 of your funds are invested for your benefit. You have already lost 5% of your money. If this sounds terrible to you, that is because it is awful. What do you get for this 5% load? Nothing. The money usually goes to a salesperson or overpaid money manager.

A back-end load is only marginally better as you pay a fee when you sell your investment. It may be explained to you that the load is charged for the privilege of being able to invest in a fund that is a superior investment. There is little or no evidence to support the assertion that load funds outperform no-load funds. The evidence supports the claim that the money lost by paying a load does not benefit the investor at all.

The investment companies that offer actively managed funds will not go down without a fight. They will do their best to convince you that you are foolish to accept the *average* performance of an index mutual fund. Mutual funds have to report their returns over 1-year, 5-year, 10-year periods and the returns since the fund's inception. They also are required to compare their performance against a benchmark index that is comparable to the fund's holdings.

Funds tend to advertise heartily when their fund has had an exceptional 1-year return. Unfortunately, research indicates that funds that do particularly well one year tend to underperform the next year. Therefore, I would urge you to ignore 1-year returns.

Five-year returns also are usually not particularly useful either. Returns since the inception of the fund are challenging to use to compare funds because funds' inception dates vary. Ten-year returns are the most useful, but they should not be the determining factor on choosing a fund. Again, it is not unusual for a mutual fund company that has dozens of funds to choose to advertise their funds that have the best ten-year returns primarily. But, just because one of their dozens of funds did well over ten years, that should engender little confidence that it is likely to repeat that performance over the next ten years.

One of my employers changed the retirement plan providers. The new provider offered dozens of stock mutual funds from various mutual fund companies. Some were low-cost index funds, and some were actively managed funds. My fellow employees and I had to choose where we wanted our retirement contributions invested.

In making my decision, I looked at the annual expense ratio and ten-year return of each fund. As expected, the index funds had the lowest annual expenses. Surprisingly, the higher annual cost actively managed funds all seemed to have 10-year returns that were higher than the index funds. But how?

I figured it out. The retirement plan provider had cherry-picked only actively managed funds that had beat the market index over the past ten years. This seemed to indicate that these funds were superior despite their higher fees. It was a mirage. The provider had thousands of actively managed funds to choose from and only chose the ones that had done exceptionally well over the past ten years, ignoring the majority that had performed well below the index fund.

This was a bit like picking winning lottery numbers after the lottery results are out. It doesn't mean those numbers are likely to win tomorrow. It just means they had won in the past.

Let's recap. For most people, investing in bond mutual funds with low fees is an easier, safer, and more practical way to invest in bonds than investing in individual bonds. For most people, investing in a no-load stock mutual fund with low annual fees is the safest and most effective way to invest in stocks. Ten-year returns are worth noticing, but low annual fees should be the overriding factor in deciding which mutual fund to choose.

Should You Start Your Own Business?

You may prefer to start your own business. Many people have undoubtedly enjoyed great financial and personal success from this path. Still, this path is risky. You must be prepared to lose your entire investment. Many successful entrepreneurs lost everything before they became a success on their second, third, or fourth attempt at starting a business. I must admit that it is not in my makeup to follow this path, but I am glad that there are entrepreneurs out there that have taken this course.

I still plan to start a business, but it will be with money I can afford to lose. If you want to start a business, I would advise you to do it while you are younger with fewer financial responsibilities. If you do, good luck. If you fail, learn from your failure and use what you learn to move towards financial success.

This book is not designed to help budding entrepreneurs. If you want to start your own business, I encourage you to do so. Still, please do your homework before you get started to increase your chances of success.

Warning! Avoid Scams.

Let's discuss some potential unwise investment decisions here because the number one thing that good investors do is to avoid scams and money-losing investments. You should never make an investment based on a cold call. That is when someone that has little or no connection with you tries to sell you an investment. These are usually touted as "can't miss" investments. If the investment they are selling is such an excellent opportunity, knowledgeable investors would be flocking to them. They would not need to be knocking on doors, calling, and emailing strangers. Just say, "no."

Multi-level marketing that requires you to sell products to friends and recruit others rarely pays off unless you are exceptionally good at recruiting other people to sell the product. Most of us know the type of companies that use this method to make sales. I won't mention any specific names because I prefer not to have to defend myself in a lawsuit. These types of companies often sell cosmetics, jewelry, food containers, lingerie, cleaning products, and nutritional supplements. You can make some money with these arrangements. But if you are required to purchase inventory upfront, most people lose their investment. Be wary.

Financial scams are alive and well in the world. The scammers can be very sophisticated. Usually, they appear professional, trustworthy, and successful. Many financial scammers have relationships or ties that they exploit to gain their victims' trust. For example, they use religious or ethnic relations. Most of us want to trust members of our church or people that hail from our home country. The scammers know this and take advantage of it.

In general, if an investment sounds too good to be true, it almost certainly is a bad idea. It might be a total scam. For example, let's say I offered you a guaranteed 15% yearly return on your investment, whether the stock market went up or down. That is too good to be true and is a scam. This is almost precisely the same promise that Bernie Madoff made to his investors.

Bernie Madoff ran the most successful pyramid (or Ponzi) scheme of all time. The exact amount that he stole from investors is not known, but all credible estimates top $10 billion. A pyramid scheme is one in which new investors money is used to pay off earlier investors. Earlier investors brag about their successful investments, which helps to attract new investors. At some point, there are no more new investors, and the whole scheme collapses.

It took several years for Madoff's scheme to collapse. He managed to fool some famous and otherwise knowledgeable investors. Part of the reason that he was so successful was that he had a solid reputation. He had a successful career in the finance industry and had served as the Chairman of the NASDAQ stock market (at the time, the second-largest stock market in the world).

Madoff is Jewish and used his connections and trust in the Jewish community to scam many Jewish charities and individuals. This type of affinity fraud is common. It is easier for bad actors to take advantage of groups that they are a part of, such as religious or ethnic groups.

Many lessons can be learned from the Madoff scheme and similar scams. First, be very wary of anything that sounds too good to be true. Second, don't invest in anything you do not fully understand. Third, do not trust someone entirely because they appear to be respectable. Finally, don't trust someone simply because they are in a group you belong to, whether that group is religious, racial, ethnic, or another similar bond. We want to trust people that are in groups in which we have a strong bond. But we don't want to trust them with our life savings without extensive and expert due diligence.

The bottom line is that if an investment sounds too good to be true, it probably is not valid. Don't let greed drive you towards becoming a victim, especially if the person selling you the investment is not attached to a well-known and reputable financial company. Also, you should always know how someone selling an investment is getting paid and how much they are getting paid for securing your investment. They should be willing to provide this information to you. If an advisor is unwilling to inform you of how much you are paying them, do not do business with them under any circumstances.

Chapter 6: Essential Financial Tasks

TCB! That means that you should be "Taking Care of Business." Elvis Presley often used the term to refer to getting the important things done. He even named one of his backup bands," The TCB Band." "Taking Care of Business" is also a fine, rocking song by Bachman-Turner Overdrive.

I often use TCB to refer to getting the important things done. I have used the phrase to encourage my daughters to do the things they need to do to succeed. TCB is a good mantra to make sure that you don't forget the essential elements that are required for success.

In personal finance, TCB means ensuring that your insurance, will, and taxes are in order. If you do everything else correctly, but fail in one of these three areas, you have failed. That is why you need to take care of business in these crucial tasks, even if they are not particularly pleasant.

Life insurance is the ultimate euphemism. It is really death insurance, and we don't like to think about that. Still, if you have loved ones that depend on your income, you owe it to them to consider life insurance.

For most people, there are two significant questions about life insurance: What type of insurance should I get and how much coverage do I need? Let's find some answers to these questions.

If you died and no one that you care about would be hurt financially, you do not need life insurance. If your net worth is not enough to bury you, give instructions to do it cheaply, and start making money.

If you have a spouse, children, or anyone else that depends on you financially, you need to buy life insurance. Let me repeat that for emphasis. Don't let your loved ones down, get life insurance to protect them if they depend on your income. Also, a primary caregiver for children or other dependents may need life insurance. In general, children do not need life insurance. If something happens to you, your loved ones will be hurt. Don't add financial pain to their loss.

If you need life insurance, the exact amount you need depends on several factors. Factors include everyone's ages, debt level, savings, investments, and other income. Don't forget that if you pass away, your dependents will likely receive income from Social Security. Also, there will no longer be a need for your retirement savings, and income required for your monthly expenses such as transportation and food go away. Remember, you only need to replace after-tax income.

A commonly used rule of thumb for life insurance is to purchase insurance coverage equivalent to six to ten times your annual salary. You can adjust this for other factors, but I advise erring on the side of too much coverage.

There are numerous types of life insurance, but you only have to remember one. Term life insurance is pure life insurance, meaning that there is no investment component to the policy. Term life insurance is simple, you give the insurance company money, and they give your beneficiaries more money if you die. Term life insurance is the least expensive type of life insurance.

Other types of life insurance such as whole life, universal life, and variable universal life (VUL) have an investment component to them. In almost all cases, the investment component is mediocre at best and more commonly awful. It is best to stick with term life insurance. If you are rich, these types of life insurance can sometimes provide a useful tax dodge, but then again, this book is not designed for the rich. Stick with term life insurance.

Term life insurance supplies only one benefit, a payoff to your beneficiaries if you die. Therefore, it is much less expensive than life insurance options that include investment aspects. Term life insurance rates are usually quite reasonable for relatively healthy people under 50. Even if you don't fall into this age and health category, term life insurance is worth exploring if you need it.

Most people should buy level term insurance. Level term means your payments will not change during the life of the insurance, usually twenty or thirty years. Term life insurance is often available from employers for you and your spouse at very reasonable rates. You should explore this insurance option first to see if you can get a low price for your insurance. An added benefit to buying your life insurance through your employer is that the money is deducted from your pay before you see it. This removes the temptation not to pay your insurance premium, something that many people do sooner or later, which is usually a big mistake.

Term life rates are higher for older people, but that is not all bad. If you have saved money for your retirement, that money can be used to supplement life insurance. After all, if you die, you will not need that retirement money. Therefore, if you have sizable retirement savings, you do not need as much life insurance.

How much insurance do you need? If you're single, the answer may be zero. If you are married without children, the answer may still be zero, but it may not be. If you have children, you almost certainly need substantial life insurance for both parents. Stay-at-home parents provide significant benefits to the family that cannot be measured in financial terms. Still, if a stay-at-home parent is no longer there, the remaining family will need money to overcome the loss. The general rule is to have enough insurance so that your loved ones do not financially suffer if you die. They will suffer from their loss, and it is preferable not to add financial distress to this unfortunate situation.

This general rule is difficult to calculate in most instances. If you want to have a simple rule of thumb for insurance for couples with children, I suggest eight times the annual income for each parent. If only one parent works outside the home, I recommend you also insure the stay-at-home spouse for four times the yearly income of the spouse working outside the home. The differing insurance suggestions are not meant to devalue the contribution of stay-at-home parents. It is merely a recognition of the fact that many of the contributions of stay-at-home parents cannot be replaced by money.

I would much prefer that you follow this simple rule of thumb for insurance than not to have insurance at all. Still, life insurance is an important life decision, so I would advise you to try to determine a more detailed estimate of the amount of coverage you need. This will require estimating the long-term financial needs of your family if you are suddenly gone. It is not an easy calculation. You must include things like Social Security payments and lower expenses because you will not be spending money on your needs. You can find assistance in calculating your insurance needs on the internet or from a fee-only financial advisor. You should avoid sales agents that are paid on commission.

Term life insurance is an expense that you will *hopefully* be making for decades. Therefore, you should shop for your life insurance online. This will help you to avoid talking to a salesperson that is likely to try to upsell you to a whole life policy (which undoubtedly will pay them a higher commission). Some useful websites to use for comparison life insurance shopping include Insure.com, PolicyGenius.com, and Quotacy.com. Other useful websites can help you to find a proper term life insurance policy. Still, be wary because many "quote" websites are owned by insurance companies, and their goal is to funnel you to their parent company's policies.

Please don't leave your financially-dependent loved ones unprotected in case of your untimely demise. Personally, I enjoy wasting another life insurance payment every month. The alternative is collecting on the policy. I hope to avoid that for a few decades more. Still, every day is a little brighter for me because I realize that my loved ones will be provided for financially if something happens to me.

Another thing you need to do to protect your loved ones is make a will. If you do not have a will, the state will decide how your estate is distributed and who will take care of your children. That is rarely the optimal outcome. Many people assume that if they die, their spouse will inherit everything, but it often doesn't work that way and varies from state to state. Don't leave the fate of your survivors to chance and the state.

Without a proper will, changing ownership of financial accounts, cars, and real estate, and other critical legal changes are much more difficult for your wife and children. Also, wills must be filed appropriately with the correct state agency. Merely writing one out by hand or using will preparation software is usually inadequate. It is difficult to do correctly without getting a lawyer involved.

If you have a complicated will, I advise finding a lawyer that specializes in estate planning. It will not be inexpensive, but it will be worth the money to have the peace of mind of knowing that your will is prepared correctly. If you have a simple, standard type of will (everything going to your wife and children), you may be able to get the job done on the cheap using LegalZoom.com or Nolo.com. Even if you use these services to prepare the will, I advise having a local lawyer review the will and make sure it is correctly filed with the state. An invalid will is little better than no will at all. Please create a proper will so that your loved ones are not burdened with *attempting* to straighten out your affairs as they are grieving.

Much like life insurance, health insurance is a bit of a euphemism. It is primarily insurance for when you get sick. At least, disability insurance is named accurately. Still, if possible, you should have health and disability insurance. The consequences of not having these coverages if a significant health problem befalls you are just too great to ignore.

Most people know they need health insurance, but many consider disability insurance optional. I don't look at disability insurance that way. You are more likely to be disabled than to die during working years. Therefore, I think it is a good investment in peace of mind to have disability insurance.

Disability policy terms vary a great deal. Make sure you know what you are purchasing and if it will meet your needs. The best disability policies start paying 3 to 6 months after disability and pay until retirement. Make sure you know the insurance policy's definition of a disability. You should also consider your emergency savings when deciding how much disability insurance you need.

Most jobs offer health and disability insurance at rates that are better than you can get elsewhere. The laws surrounding health care are changing rapidly and are likely to change again soon. Therefore, it is not possible to give detailed specific advice on the type of insurance you need and where you should purchase your insurance. Consequently, you will need to do some homework to decide where to get your health and disability insurance. You should have both types of insurance.

Many employers offer a choice between a high-deductible and a low-deductible plan. High-deductible plans usually have lower monthly premiums, but higher out-of-pocket costs if you need medical services. Conversely, low-deductible plans typically have higher monthly premiums but lower out-of-pocket costs if you need medical services.

There are rules of thumb as to which type of plan you should choose. Generally, if you are healthy and have the money saved to pay unexpected medical expenses, you should select a high-deductible plan. If you expect to need extensive medical care, a low-deductible plan is probably your best option.

Long-term care insurance is problematic. Costs are extremely high and getting higher as life spans increase, and the number of people needing prohibitively expensive long-term care increases. Also, most long-term care insurance does not pay for the first 90 days of care. Furthermore, long-term care insurance often only covers a portion of costs. Short-term care insurance is a less expensive option, but coverage is usually capped at one year. Medicaid is another option, but the government is required to recover as much of the cost of care as possible from the estate of the person receiving care. One option that is not recommended is planning on using family for long-term care. The stress can be enormous and can damage family relations.

The sorry state of the long-term care situation has led to a search for better solutions from governments and the healthcare and insurance industries. Hopefully, better options will be created. In the meantime, you should make a plan for this situation once you are in your fifties or sixties.

Health and disability insurance are essential financial components that should be considered when you are deciding where you want to be employed. Usually, a job with lower pay and employer-subsidized health and disability insurance is preferred to a job that offers somewhat higher pay and no insurance. It is certainly something to consider when you are deciding between two positions.

Insurance is a drag. You must pay for something that you hope you never use. If you are borrowing money to purchase a home or auto, you will most likely be required to buy insurance. Being forced to buy something that you hope you never use is just a big bummer. Still, if you ever need home or auto insurance, you are going to be glad that you have the coverage.

In the case of homeowner's and automobile insurance, choosing a high-deductible policy will decrease the premium you pay. That's good. A higher deductible means that you will have to pay more if there is damage to your property that is covered by the insurance. That's bad. On the other hand, a higher deductible means you are likely to make fewer claims against your insurance (if the damage is below the deductible limit). Fewer claims generally leads to lower rates and a lower likelihood that your policy will be canceled. That's good.

There is a trade-off, but I generally recommend buying a high-deductible policy for your homeowner and automobile insurance. The savings are substantial, and hopefully, you will never have to pay the deductible. For this plan to work, you must have the money in reserve that would need to be paid in case you have damage that requires you to pay the deductible.

If you rent your domicile, you may need renter's insurance. You should consider renter's insurance if you have furniture and other belongings that you could not afford to replace if you are the victim of fire, theft, or some other disaster. Homeowners' insurance may not cover certain things such as floods, earthquake, sinkholes, jewelry, or other expensive personal items. You need to be sure of what is included in your policy.

You should take a video of your house every year or two and store it somewhere outside of your home (outside online storage will work). Walk from room to room (including attics, basements, and closets), getting a video shot of every valuable item while including audio descriptions. If you have a covered disaster in your home, this video will greatly aid you in being reimbursed for your loss.

The most important thing to know about automobile and homeowner insurance is that you should shop around. Rates can vary significantly from company to company for the same or similar coverage. Furthermore, you should shop around every few years and make sure your coverage is adequate. If your home's value doubles over time, but your insurance coverage does not, you may not be able to buy a similar home if your home is destroyed.

Insurance is a reoccurring expense. Therefore, the importance of managing this expense is increased. Make sure you are adequately covered by insurance but pay as little as you can for the coverage you need.

Here is a confession: I don't enjoy paying taxes. In fact, I would greatly prefer to pay far fewer taxes. Some people would think this makes me unpatriotic. I think this makes me a typical American. Also, I am a military veteran, and I consider myself quite patriotic. I love America. I just don't like paying *more* than my fair share.

Here is some advice for my fellow Americans that don't want to pay too much in taxes. Do not make foolish financial decisions simply to avoid taxes. Many people invest in legal and ethical tax shelters or tax-advantaged investments to avoid taxes. Also, many of these investors do not realize that they are giving up potentially higher after-tax returns in other investments.

If you invest primarily to take advantage of a tax break and the tax break goes away (as they often do), you may find yourself stuck in an investment with sub-par returns and no tax advantage.

Tax preferred investments that encourage saving for retirement or college include IRAs, 401(k)s, 403(b)s, 457s, and 529s. These types of tax-preferred investments are almost always excellent investment opportunities with significant long-term tax advantages.

The tax code and temporarily tax-advantaged investments are ever-changing. Don't make crucial long-term investment decisions based on these criteria. After all, the easiest way to avoid taxes is to make zero money. We don't want to do that.

Paying income taxes is not all bad; it means you're making money. Still, taxes can be painful. In some states like New York and California, many residents take home less than 50% of their income after paying federal, state, and local taxes. Ouch!

On the other hand, approximately half of wage earners pay zero federal income tax after they file their returns. All in all, paying federal income tax is a good thing because it means you have a healthy income. Of course, there are lots of other taxes. Sales tax, local income tax, property tax, FICA (social security and Medicare) are just some of the different taxes that most people pay.

There are two basic types of income tax rates, average and marginal. Your average tax rate is the percentage of your total income that you pay in income tax. For example, if you make $100,000 a year and you pay $20,000 in income taxes, you have an average tax rate of 20% because $20,000 divided by $100,000 is 20% (sorry for the math).

Your marginal tax rate is the rate that you pay on your next dollar of income. As you earn more, your marginal tax rate goes up. Your marginal tax rate is often called your tax bracket. If you are trying to decide if it is worth it to earn some extra cash, your marginal tax rate is the one that matters. Let's say you are thinking of making an additional $100 this weekend, and your marginal tax rate is 30%. This means you will have to pay a tax of 30% on your $100, leaving you 70% or $70 of the pay as take-home pay. This simple example does not include other taxes or deductions related to your income.

Your marginal tax bracket can be found in tax software or by a tax preparer. You can also find this information on the internet. Tax brackets change quite often because the federal government changes them quite often. Typically, the highest federal income tax bracket is between 35% to 40%. This does not include state, local, and other taxes.

There are many examples in the past of people taking extraordinary measures to avoid taxes. Unfortunately, the surest way to avoid taxes is not to make any money. Many tax-avoidance schemes eventually boil down to this, losing money. That is not a smart way to avoid taxes. In general, it is best to make as much money as you can while taking prudent steps to avoid unnecessary tax payments.

Filing your taxes yearly is a pain, but it must be done. I skipped filing my taxes for two years when I was overseas in the military in the eighties. Dumb! I would have almost certainly received a return of a few hundred dollars each year (1980s dollars!). There are only two possibilities when you do not file your taxes. Either you are foregoing a tax return (bad), or you owe money that you are not paying (worse). The penalties for not filing a tax return include fines, high-interest payments, a criminal record, and jail time. As I said, file your taxes every year.

Hopefully, filling out tax forms will get easier as the federal government simplifies taxes in the coming years. Of course, I have been hoping that for decades. No luck so far. If you are not buying a home, don't have your own business, and don't have children, there is an excellent chance you can fill out your tax form with ease.

If you might benefit from itemizing your deductions, it is almost certainly a good idea to use tax preparation software or a tax professional to file your tax return. I have been using tax software to prepare my taxes for over 20 years. If you use one of the most popular tax preparation software brands, it is not a particularly complicated process. Most tax preparation software will store your personal information for the next year. This makes it significantly easier to prepare your taxes using the software the following year.

There are many reputable, competent tax professionals available to help you complete your returns. Unfortunately, tax preparation professionals have a perverse incentive that may hurt you. Monetarily speaking, the primary motivation for tax preparers is to fill out your tax return in a way that is the least likely to get you audited or to end up paying penalties or interest for underpayment of taxes. That is fine, but another way to put this is that they have no financial motivation to search for tax deductions that you are entitled to receive.

If you are audited or fined, the tax preparer is often on the hook for these mistakes. If they save you money by judiciously taking all the deductions that they see fit, they get no financial reward. These facts do not mean that you should not use a tax preparation professional. They do suggest that you should be involved and review the returns that the professional made for you.

Right after I married my beautiful Bride, we used her Father's accountant to prepare our taxes as she had since becoming an adult. I did not want to rock the boat. As it turns out, I had the most complicated tax return I had ever had that year because I had cashed in some stock options from my employer. I reviewed the return the accountant had prepared. Essentially, I did the return calculations a second time. I discovered an error that would have caused me to pay $10,000 more in taxes than I needed to pay. I filed the tax return I had prepared, saved myself $10,000, and never used that accountant again. I don't believe the accountant was incompetent. I think the accountant did not have any financial incentive to ensure that I was paying the minimum tax that I was required to pay.

Give to Charity; It Will Improve Your Life

Money is *not* the root of all evil. The familiar quote, "money is the root of all evil," from the Bible (1 Timothy 6:10) is taken out of context. The actual quote taken from the NIV version of the bible is "the love of money is the root of all kinds of evil." Well, Christian or not, it is hard to argue with that.

Still, you don't have to be evil to make money, even if you make lots of it. The primary point of this book is to help you to make lots of money, otherwise known as becoming rich. Lots of wealthy people have garnered great wealth and used that wealth to help others. Andrew Carnegie, one of the richest men of the early 1900s, donated enough money to build over 2,500 libraries. He said, "the man who dies rich dies disgraced." He dedicated his last years to giving away most of his fortune.

Philanthropy from the rich still endures. Warren Buffett and Bill Gates, two men that are among the richest in the world, have pledged to give almost all their wealth to charity. Over 150 other billionaires have signed onto the "Giving Pledge" and promised to donate over half of their wealth to charity (perhaps posthumously).

Whether you follow the advice in this book or not, you are very unlikely to garner the wealth of a Buffett or Gates. If you can find a book that tells you how to do that, let me know. Still, I hope that as you become rich and after you become rich, you will spend some effort and money helping others. Do it for yourself as much as others. A leader at a church that I used to attend often said, "don't give until it hurts; give until it feels good." That is probably my favorite quote about charity, and I try to take it to heart.

No, making money is not inherently evil, especially if you use a substantial portion of that money to help others. Despite the awful portrayals of wealthy people in just about every movie or TV show, most of the wealthy people I have met tend to be very concerned with giving back to society. I will not advise you to do anything unethical or illegal. Please don't.

I want to emphasize here again that giving your time or money to charity is something you should do. You should pick a charity and cause you know to be worthy. That way, you know your money will be spent to actually help people and not just end up in some fundraiser's pocket.

As your wealth increases, you should have the resources to give more to charity.

Everyone should give money to or volunteer for charities or both. If you are a good person, helping charities will benefit you. It should feel good to help other people. You should actively plan how much money and time to give. Charitable giving should be a line item in your budget. Your plan should have flexibility. Of course, the plan is only useful if you use it. Reevaluate your plan at least once a year.

It is much easier to effectively give to a very few or even just one charity. Look for charities that inspire you to give, and that work on a cause that you believe is worthy. Volunteer for charities where you think you are likely to meet people that will encourage you to volunteer more.

Do your due diligence. Don't give to charities you have not checked out. Don't give just because a charity has called, mailed, emailed, came up to you on the street, or otherwise gotten in your face. Always check out a charity before you give. Remember, any dollar you give to an ineffective or corrupt charity is a dollar you cannot donate to an effective charity.

Many legal charities use only a small percentage of donations for stated goals. Legally, a charity may spend almost all of its funds raised on expenses such as employee and management salaries, overhead expenses, and fundraising. It is preferable to donate money and time to charities that are highly efficient at raising money and giving to their stated goal. Many charities have somewhat misleading names. Therefore, you should make sure you agree with your chosen charity's stated purpose.

There are many places to research the quality of charities. Two useful websites are charitywatch.org/top-rated-charities and charitynavigator.org. Many religion-related charities are not rated. That does not mean that they are not wonderful charities. For example, The Salvation Army is an exceptional charity and one of my favorites.

Many smaller charities are not rated. There is one easy way to check out smaller charities. If a small charity has major corporate partners, that is an excellent sign that they are a legitimate charity. Most major corporations have people dedicated to checking out the charities that the corporation helps. The corporation wants to garner favorable publicity from its charitable giving and wants to avoid giving money to a scam charity.

Publicize that you give to charity (especially if you do so through your business). This action will educate and remind others about good charities. It can inspire others to get involved and to give. It is okay if people think you are a good person doing good things.

If you can take advantage of the tax benefits of giving to charity, do so. Keep your receipts and write them off on your taxes. Don't think of this as being selfish. Tax benefits may allow you to give more to charity. That is a good thing. For example, if you itemize your taxes and you are in the 20% income tax bracket, you can donate $1.00 to charity or donate $0.80 to charity and pay $0.20 in taxes. If your goal is to help people, then you can help more by taking advantage of tax breaks.

The level of giving is up to you. Still, giving money or donating your time should make you feel good about doing good and it should thusly improve your life. The first time that I met my wife was when we were working a charity event for foster children. We helped some kids and some families that day, but we helped ourselves even more even though that was not our primary goal. It has been my experience that giving time and money to charity benefits me as much or more than it does the ones I am helping.

A Good Financial Advisor is a Godsend; A Bad Financial Advisor is a Vampire

I have known many people that did not understand their finances. Many of them reasoned that this was okay because they had a financial advisor. They did not understand or ignored the fact that financial advisors are first and foremost sales professionals. If a salesperson gets paid on commission, they have an incentive to generate more commissions. Therefore, they may not be primarily concerned with how well your investments do. For this reason, most other financial experts and I recommend that you use a fee-only financial advisor.

If you are not yet wealthy, it may *not* be a good idea to use a fee-only financial advisor. The fee for such advisors usually ranges from $500 to several thousand dollars per year. If they are talented and trustworthy advisors and you have substantial investments, this is money well spent.

If you have less than $100,000 to invest, a fee-only financial advisor might not make sense. In this case, financial advisors that receive a portion of the money you invest or earn on your investment can be a reasonable choice. As long as a commission-based financial advisor is upfront about how they are compensated for the investment they are advising you to make, they can be beneficial.

The primary job of a financial advisor should not only be to provide you with sound financial advice. The advisor should also help you to understand your investments and how the financial advisor is compensated. If the advisor is offering you valuable guidance, they should not be ashamed to explain how they are paid and why they deserve it.

It is a good idea to hire people to help you with your financial decisions: tax accountants, real estate agents, estate lawyers, and a Certified Financial Planner™. Still, you should not blindly trust them, and you should know how they are compensated and what service they are providing you. You must understand your finances, any advice you receive, and the impact of the financial decisions you are making.

Don't make the mistake of trusting a financial advisor blindly simply because they work for a reputable big-name bank or financial company. Also, don't trust a company simply because they have a paid celebrity spokesperson that you admire. The representative of a reputable financial organization is indeed much less likely to commit fraud, embezzle your funds, or outright rip you off.

On the other hand, they can legally and ethically offer you costly advice which is sub-standard. Some financial advisors earn more from their customers' investments than the customers do. Yikes! Don't let that happen to you. Make sure you know how and how much your financial advisor earns.

If you do not understand an investment, don't make it. You should be able to explain to a 12-year-old why you are making a financial decision. Complicated is bad. If you have a financial advisor, he or she should be able to explain why a decision is a good idea and how he or she is paid to you. If you don't understand, the choice is too complicated and problematic.

When you first get started on your plan for financial success, you probably won't need a financial planner. As your wealth increases, say over $100,000, consulting a fee-only Certified Financial Planner™ will start to make sense. Indeed, you should learn about financial matters by reading information regularly. Financial laws, economic factors, and personal financial situations change continually. So there is no such thing as knowing everything you will ever need to know about finance. Still, having a trusted, trained, fee-only financial planner is a great idea for almost everyone at some point.

As I approached financial security, I decided to turn my hobby into my career. I loved reading about personal financial management. I decided that all I needed to launch a new career in my chosen field was academic credentials to enhance the knowledge I already possessed.

I had dreamed of working as an investment manager while working for over a decade as a systems analyst. In my spare time, I never read about the latest computer language or how to better manage a software project. No, I was an investment junkie. I read the *Wall Street Journal* daily, *Barron's* weekly, and *Forbes* as soon as it came in the mail. I earned a master's in finance with a 4.0 GPA from one of the most respected southern business universities (Go Panthers!). Although I got an excellent education while earning my Masters, my degree was just a formality. My real education came from reading these three publications and the occasional book about financial management or investments.

I passed the Level 1 examination of the Chartered Financial Analyst program on the first try, something that most experienced financial analysts fail to do. I felt I had prepared for a transition into the investment management field. I was foolishly naïve.

What I repeatedly heard while applying for jobs that involved giving financial advice to the public was "we don't hire finance majors" to provide financial advice. Wait, what now? I found out that what the financial advice firms wanted to hire were good salespeople. They need to know a little about finance, but they don't necessarily need to be experts. There are experts back at corporate that will decide what they want to be sold, and the financial advisors will sell the products. That is how most financial advice firms work. Most of these firms had found that finance majors were not good salespeople and, perish the thought, often offered their point of view on investments.

It is crucial to keep in mind that financial advisors and stockbrokers are first and foremost salespeople. Most financial advisors sell whatever earns them the highest commission and what has done well lately (what corporate tells them to sell). There is nothing inherently wrong with financial advisors wanting to make as much money as they legally and ethically can. Still, you need to be aware of their goals so that you can look out for your interests. Also, it is generally better to follow the advice of a well-paid financial advisor than to not plan, invest, and save at all.

Still, remember that a financial advisor is not necessarily your friend. Hopefully, if you ever choose to have a financial advisor, you will select one that is trustworthy and pleasant, but your relationship is a business one. By the way, almost any good financial advisor (salesperson) will present themselves as your friend. It is a great way to get a sale. But *caveat emptor*, that's Latin for "don't be a sucker."

Let me use an analogy to drive home my point. It is common for customers of a financial advisor to enter the advisor's office and say, "tell me what I need to do." They also rarely ask what costs, fees, and commissions are involved in different types of investments. The same people that make this kind of mistake would never think of going onto a car lot and telling the salesman, "tell me what I need to buy." They know the car salesperson will do what is best for the car salesperson. Namely, sell the sucker the most expensive car they can afford (or almost afford) with the highest interest rate loan and the highest commission. Almost everyone knows that they must be wary of a car salesperson's motives. But few people know they should be suspicious of financial products salesperson's motives.

Therefore, it is probably a great idea to think of financial advisors as salespeople. That way you will be wary. It doesn't mean you shouldn't try to build trust with a financial product salesperson. It does mean you should understand their motives and goals.

Now, if you are doing quite well financially or need estate or trust advice, seeking the counsel of a qualified financial advisor is an excellent idea. You should start with a fee-only Certified Financial Planner™ (CFP®) that is a member of NAPFA. The National Association of Personal Financial Advisors (NAPFA) is the country's leading professional association of Fee-Only financial advisors.

Reputable investment advisors follow one of two major standards. NAPFA members adhere to a *fiduciary standard*, which means the advisor puts clients' interests first. Advisors that operate under the fiduciary standard must disclose and *avoid* any conflicts of interest. It would be a conflict of interest if the advisor put a client in an investment that is not the best for the client but pays the advisor a healthy commission or fee.

Many advisors, brokers and insurance agents adhere to a *suitability standard*. This standard is less strenuous. It allows advisors to sell investments to clients that are suitable (okay) for a client, while not disclosing conflicts of interest that incentivize the advisor to bypass better investments. Generally, you should stick with advisors that follow the *fiduciary standard* and always know how your advisor earns all their money. If they will not disclose all of their income from your business, you don't want to do business with them.

Fee-only means that the advisor is paid a flat fee and does not receive commissions for the investments they advise you to make. This way, their only incentive is to give you good advice so that you will return and recommend them to your friends. It is rare to find an advisor that has a flat fee of less than $500. But if you have reached a point in your life where you need their advice, it can be money extremely well-spent.

I am not a registered financial advisor. I possess a Ph.D. in Business Administration with a concentration in Finance, and I have taught finance, including investments and personal financial planning at two universities for over a decade. I am not a Certified Financial Planner™ (CFP®), but I did pass the educational requirements and the certification exam. I chose to spend the time and money to accomplish this so that I could have the confidence that my advice was sound.

I am not planning to seek a CFP® certification because there is an extensive experience requirement. I am not willing to quit my academic and writing career to become a full-time financial planner. That is not all bad because I can give you advice that does not adhere to the guidelines of the CFP® certifying organization.

I believe that their advice, while sound and reliable, does tend to be too conservative. The reason for this is simple. If you give conventional financial advice, you are unlikely to get sued. Generally, if the financial advisors adhere to the guidelines, they will be protected in a lawsuit. The guidelines usually do not protect investors from overpriced, mediocre, or even sub-par advice.

Still, I'd advise you to look for certifications in financial advisors because it is an excellent minimum bar. You would not want a doctor without a medical degree. Similarly, you don't want a paid financial advisor without a stamp of approval from the organization that monitors their industry. Just keep in mind that a certification does not *guarantee* you will receive quality advice.

Chapter 7: Plan for Retirement, Start Early

Start Planning for Retirement Today. Yes, Today!

The primary goal of saving for retirement is to save enough to have your savings reach a level of critical mass. "Critical mass" means that your retirement savings are earning more each year than you are withdrawing. If you reach critical mass, you will never run out of money. Achieving critical mass is a lofty goal, but it should be your goal.

Don't rely on life expectancy statistics to determine how much money you will need. If your life expectancy at retirement is 12 years and you save accordingly, living 30 years could become a problem. My wife's grandmother used to say, "getting old is not for wimps." Getting old without sufficient income can be terrible.

Some version of Social Security will almost certainly be around when you retire, even if you are very young. You should not rely on receiving substantial income from Social Security when you retire. Some people have compared Social Security in its current form to a Ponzi scheme. There is some validity to this argument, but Social Security is a government-mandated version of a Ponzi scheme that can compel new participants to invest. That makes it much more reliable.

The economics of the social security system has changed dramatically over the years. In 1960, five workers supported one retiree. In 2010, it was three workers for each retiree. This number is expected to drop to two workers in the next twenty years. Retirees are living longer, and the full benefits retirement age has increased from 65 to 67. Social Security is going to change in the future. The most likely changes will be further increases in the retirement age and reduced benefits.

The bottom line is that Social Security income will probably provide only a poverty-level income for most recipients in the future. Currently, many retirees that rely on Social Security for all or almost all of their income live in poverty. This fact highlights the importance of saving money above and beyond the amount you are compelled to contribute to the Social Security system.

Deciding when to begin collecting Social Security benefits is a complicated decision that depends on many factors such as marital status, age, spouse's age, health, spouse's health, life expectancy, ability to work, and income needs. Whew, that is a lot! If you begin taking your benefits early, you will have a smaller monthly income, but you will receive this income for longer. Many people have decided to take reduced benefits from early retirement and then go on to live long lives with that reduced income. In other words, they lived long enough to regret their decision to retire early considerably.

As you approach age 62, you should begin formulating a plan for when you and your spouse want to start drawing Social Security retirement benefits. Of course, there are numerous sources of information on the internet. Still, if you do not feel confident in your ability to make this decision, paid professional advice might be an option worth the money.

You should start saving for your retirement when you are young. The younger, the better. My oldest daughter is searching for her first job this year. I have advised her to start contributing to her retirement plan at age 16 if she gets a job with an employer that has a matching 401(k) plan. She laughed at first, but after I explained to her the beauty of a 401(k) plan with an employer matching contribution, she said, "I'm in."

Simply put, a 401(k), 403(b), or 457 retirement plan with employer matching contributions is an unbelievably good investment and the surest way to long-term wealth building. I will explain more about this later, but first, I want to get back to a fundamental approach to avoid being poor and getting rich slowly.

Most people will not start saving for retirement in their teens, but they should. Many people do not start saving for retirement in their twenties, but they almost definitely should. A substantial number of people do not start saving for retirement until they are in their forties or fifties. Yikes, that is way too late!

Starting your retirement savings early creates several advantages for you. If you start your savings in a qualified retirement plan such as a 401(k), 403(b), 457, or individual retirement account (IRA), you usually receive substantial tax advantages. Depending on the plan, your contributions to your retirement savings may be made before taxes. That means that you will not have to pay income tax on the amount of income that you choose to contribute to your retirement.

That is a huge deal! Let's say you are in the 20% income tax bracket. In this case, if you earn an extra $1.00 before-tax, you will receive $0.80 of income after-taxes. If you decide to contribute this dollar to your tax-deferred retirement plan instead, you get the whole dollar with no taxes deducted deposited into your retirement account. This retirement account investment will then grow without taxes (tax-deferred) until you retire.

Let's clarify the options in this situation. Option 1: take the dollar, which is only 80 cents after-tax, and either spend the money or invest it and pay taxes on any investment gains immediately. Option 2: put the whole dollar into a retirement account where it will grow tax-deferred for decades until you take it out in retirement (you will have to pay taxes on the income you receive in retirement). The person that takes option two will get more money; the money will grow more quickly because it is growing tax-deferred, and taxes will only have to be paid decades later. I will take option two, and, in most circumstances, you should too.

If you are not still in your twenties and you have not started saving for your retirement, do not panic. Do get to work on making up for lost time. Don't save until it hurts. Save until it feels good. It may not feel good at first, but over time seeing your retirement account grow should give you a great feeling about what you have accomplished.

Many people claim they cannot save for retirement. Reasons include paying off student loans, are purchasing their first home, raising kids, caring for elderly parents, and on and on. Then, they wake up one morning and realize they are in their forties or fifties, and they have no retirement savings.

It becomes challenging to make up for the lost time that late in the game. Still, if you or someone you know is in that predicament, it is time to get cracking. Some lost ground can be made up through proper planning, working more, saving more, and retiring later. Better to retire with some savings than none at all.

If you must decide between saving for your retirement or saving for your children's education, it is almost always better to save for your retirement. If you save money for your kid's education, this tends to reduce the number of scholarships and loans they can receive to pay for their college. This perverse system punishes those that save for their children's education, but that is our system.

On the other hand, if you put money into your retirement account, that rarely diminishes the amount of financial aid your children can receive for college. Also, you can use retirement money to help with education if you must. There may be some penalties associated with appropriating retirement funds for educational costs. Importantly, saving for your retirement will help to relieve your children of the burden of caring for you in your old age.

If your employer offers a 401(k), 403(b) or 457 plan with an employer matching contribution, you should participate in the plan up to the amount your employer will match. I know of no better long-term investment than a retirement plan with an employer match. The reason is simple. When you participate in these plans, you are essentially getting free money. Let me explain.

What is a 401(k) or 403(b) or 457 plan? They are very similar. A 401(k) plan can be offered by an employer that is trying to make a profit. A 403(b) plan can be used by a non-profit employer such as a school, charity, or church. A government employer offers a 457 plan. Other similar plans go by names such as the Thrift Savings Plan (TSP) offered to federal employees.

Otherwise, these plans are so similar that I will only address 401(k) plans for most of the rest of the book. Still, know that if you have access to a 403(b) or 457 plan, the information and advice about 401(k) plans applies to your plan.

A 401(k) plan is a retirement plan that many employers and almost all major employers offer to their employees. Employees can automatically have a portion of their pay contributed to the 401(k) plan either before or after taxes are withheld. Earnings in the plan accrue on a tax-deferred basis. This means you do not have to pay any taxes on the gains on your investments in the plan until you withdraw money from your account (hopefully, after you retire).

Most employers will match a certain amount of the contributions that an employee makes into the plan. That is where the "free money" comes into the equation.

Employers have a lot of flexibility on the level of matching contributions that they choose to contribute to their employees' plans. Employers do not have to match anything, and some choose this path. Employers can be extremely generous. The best match I ever got from one of my employers was a matching contribution of 90 cents for each dollar that I contributed up 10% of my total pay.

The most common employer matching contribution is 50 cents for each dollar the employee contributes, with a limit of up to 6% of the employee total pay. Since this is the most common, let's use this as an example to show what a great deal a 401(k) can be. Also, to make the math simpler, let's use a person making $100,000 a year and assume they are in the 20% income tax bracket.

Let's also assume that the person contributes their money pre-tax (which is almost always the best option for 401(k) contributions). The person will be depositing $6,000, which is 6% of $100,000 every year. Since the company is matching 50 cents on the dollar, the company will contribute half of this, $3,000. So, our hypothetical person has saved a total of $9,000 in a year, including $3,000 of "free money." That's not bad for a year's savings.

Now, let's take a look at what would happen if our hypothetical worker decided to not contribute to the 401(k) plan, but instead chose to take the $6,000 and spend it or invest it elsewhere. First of all, they will not get the full $6,000 because it will be taxed at our assumed 20% tax rate. In this case, the person only receives $4,800 after taxes.

So, there are two choices in this scenario. We can have $9,000 in our retirement savings plan, or we can spend $4,800 this year. Therefore, if we choose to take the money now, we will be $4,200 poorer. That doesn't seem wise.

But wait, it gets worse. The money that we have invested in our retirement plan grows tax-deferred until retirement. That will make it increase much more quickly over time. On the other hand, if we choose to take some of the $4,800 that we received and invest it, we will have to pay taxes on any income the investment earns.

It seems like a no-brainer to take the $9,000 over the $4,800. Yet, every day for year after year, many otherwise intelligent people choose to continue to take the $4,800 over the $9,000. Logically, someone would have to be in incredibly dire straits financially to accept the lower amount.

If you make more or less money or are in a different tax bracket or have a different match or contribution percentage, the lesson does not change. You will benefit significantly from contributing to your 401(k) plan up to the level that your employer will match. Otherwise, you are throwing away "free money" and substantial tax benefits.

To emphasize the importance of this decision, let's take a look at this same example, but assume that the 401(k) match was equivalent to the best plan I ever had. In this plan, my employer would match 90 cents to the dollar for every contribution made up to 10% of my salary.

In this case, 10% of the salary of $100,000 would be $10,000. Sparing you the math, now the choice is to contribute $10,000 to your retirement and get $19,000 or take the money and get $8,000 after tax.

It seems like a simple choice. The options are to put $19,000 into your retirement fund or take home $8,000. Now, I will tell you that the best retirement plan I ever had was at a university. Also, I knew many brilliant people, including genius professors that decided that they could not afford to save the $19,000, so they took the $8,000. They were passing up $11,000 of free money a year.

It seems insane, but their rationale was I need the money now. Still, a person needs to find a way to take advantage of this "free money," tax-deferred investment returns, and this surest path to getting rich slowly.

So few people were taking advantage of 401(k) plans that the law was changed to allow employers to auto-enroll employees in their retirement plans. Many employers now do this. The number of employees contributing to 401(k) plans rose substantially with this change, but there is a problem.

The auto-enrollment contribution rates are usually quite low, often just 1% of pay. Employees that accept this auto-rate, as many do, are saving too little for retirement. Also, they are leaving scads of "free money" on the table if they do not contribute up to the level that their employer will match.

Do _not_ blindly accept the auto-enrollment rate. Make sure you are contributing as much money as your employer will match. Don't turn down "free money."

What if you are self-employed or your employer does not offer a retirement plan? The good news is that there are tax-advantaged alternatives. The bad news is that there will be no matching funds or "free money." Even worse, you have to be motivated to save on your own, the horrors. Still, it is a sage move to begin contributing to a retirement fund early in your career.

There are a few different choices for retirement savings if you do not have access to a 401(k) or 403(b) plan. If you are self-employed or own your own business, you can set up a Solo 401(k) or SEP IRA. SEP IRA is an acronym for Simplified Employee Pension Individual Retirement Account. You can contribute to a SEP IRA even if you contribute towards a 401(k) as part of your day job. Small employers may set up a Simple Individual Retirement Account (Simple IRA) for their employees and make contributions to these plans.

Anyone can contribute money to an Individual Retirement Account (IRA). This type of account is typically called a Traditional IRA. Also, anyone can contribute to a Roth IRA account as long as they don't make too much money. Additionally, a Health Savings Account (HSA) is another way to save money for medical expenses and retirement.

If this all sounds complicated, well, it is quite so. Still, it is vital to find out which retirement plan option is best for you either through research or professional advice. The alternative of doing nothing is simply unacceptable and will not end well.

I will not go into great detail about the Solo 401(k), SEP IRA, and Simple IRA because these plans are set up by small business owners. If you are a small business owner, you should have access to the expertise or financial advice to properly implement one of these plans for your benefit and the benefit of your employees. If you are an employee of a small firm that uses one of these plans, maximize the benefit from your participation, whether that be from making contributions, choosing investments, or other decisions.

I will go into greater detail about Traditional and Roth IRAs because these plans are available to almost everyone. There are many differences between these two types of plans. I will cover some of the significant differences, but the laws governing these types of accounts may change in any year. Therefore, you must make yourself aware of the latest regulations as you start, contribute, or withdraw from one of these plans.

An IRA is an investment account that you open at a financial institution such as a bank, brokerage, or mutual fund company. Opening an IRA is a somewhat straightforward process that is not much more complicated than opening a bank account. Once you decide where you want to open an IRA, you contact the financial institution where you want to open the IRA.

You use the money that you contribute to the account to purchase investments such as stocks, bonds, and mutual funds. The recurring fees charged and investment options available from various financial institutions differ significantly. Therefore, choosing an institution that offers low fees and superior investment options is very important. I recommend The Vanguard Group (vanguard.com), Charles Schwab (schwab.com), and Fidelity (fidelity.com). There are other great IRA providers out there, but Vanguard is where I have mine, my wife's and my Mom's.

The main difference between a Roth and Traditional IRA is the tax treatment of contributions and withdrawals. The income that you use to contribute to a Roth IRA is not tax-deductible (you have to pay taxes on the income). On the other hand, when you withdraw money from a Roth IRA, you do not have to pay taxes on the money you withdraw. The beauty of this is that income that your contributions earn while in the Roth IRA is never taxed.

The income that you use to contribute to a Traditional IRA is tax-deductible. Income withdrawn from a Traditional IRA is taxed. Still, your initial contribution provides a tax break, and your investments in the Traditional IRA grow tax-deferred until you withdraw them.

As of 2019, the yearly contribution limit to an IRA (either Roth or Traditional) is $6,000 if you are under 50 years old and $7,000 if you are 50 or older. As of 2019, the contribution amount that a single person and married couple (filing jointly) could make to a Roth IRA was phased out beginning at income levels of $122,000 and $193,000, respectively. If you take money out of a Traditional or Roth IRA before age 59 ½, you will have to pay a 10% federal tax penalty (except under certain hardship conditions). Still, an IRA is an excellent retirement savings choice for those that do not have access to a better plan, such as a 401(k) with an employer match.

Choosing between a Traditional or Roth IRA is difficult because to make the absolutely correct decision, you have to be able to predict the future. Simply put, if you think your current tax rate is higher than the one you will pay in retirement, choose a Traditional IRA. Otherwise, choose a Roth IRA. Selecting the right option requires a knowledge of your future income level, which is not entirely predictable, and future tax rates (good luck with that).

In my case, I have decided to punt. I have most of my retirement savings in a Traditional IRA and a significant portion of my retirement savings in a Roth IRA. That way, I can manage my income and taxes in retirement by choosing which account to withdraw from in any given year. Managing retirement contribution choices to perfection is difficult. Still, contributing to a retirement program early and often with some diligent planning is likely to pay off during your golden years.

I read a brilliant piece of advice in my early twenties. I wish I could give credit to the source of this impactful advice, but, much like most of my twenties, my knowledge of the source is long gone.

The advice was simple. At the start of your career, find a way to invest enough in your company's 401(k) to garner all of the employer matching contributions available to you. Secondly, every time you get a raise (which tends to happen more often early in your career), use half of that raise to increase your retirement savings contributions and the other half to improve your lifestyle.

The beauty of this advice is you don't miss the money you contribute to your 401(k) at the start of your career. You have just left school, and you are making more than you ever have before anyway. You don't miss the half of your raises that are going to increased retirement contributions because the other half of the raise is going towards improving your lifestyle.

Life gets better as your finances improve. Ooh, la, la!

I took this advice, and it worked magnificently for me. My lifestyle improved steadily, and my retirement savings increased tremendously. Three years after I completed college, I was contributing 15% (the maximum allowed in my 401(k) at the time) of my salary pre-tax into my retirement account. My company was matching a portion of that to bring my total savings to 19% of my pre-tax salary.

Additionally, these retirement savings were earning income tax-deferred. The growth in my retirement savings was phenomenal. I could have comfortably retired in my fifties if I had not gotten the crazy idea to go back to school full-time to earn my doctorate in finance. Still, my savings largely supported me, my wife, and two small children during my six years of graduate study. My experience is an excellent testament to the advantages of starting your savings early and saving as much as possible while still enjoying life.

Many people have told me that they do not want to contribute to a 401(k) plan because if they have to take their money out before age 59 ½, they will have to pay income tax on the withdrawal plus a 10% penalty on the income. In most situations, early withdrawal from a retirement account will result in taxes owed plus a 10% penalty. There are certain exceptions on early withdrawal penalties related to extensive medical and housing expenses and education costs.

Still, it is usually a poor decision to avoid saving for retirement to escape the possibility of a penalty later. If you get an employer match on your savings, you have even more incentive to begin saving for retirement immediately. Let's say you have a 50% match. If you don't contribute to your 401(k) to avoid a potential penalty, you are passing up an immediate 50% return on your investment to avoid a possible 10% penalty later. That is not a logical decision because you will still finish way ahead after you pay the penalty. This calculation does not even include any earnings your retirement savings earn over time. In short, it doesn't make sense to avoid contributing to your retirement savings to avoid taking money out early later on. Still, it is best to keep retirement savings in your retirement account until you retire.

Many companies offer the option to you to borrow from your 401(k) plan. I strongly recommend that you do not exercise this option if it is available to you. Borrowing from your 401(k) sounds fine on the surface. You can borrow the money and use it for anything, and then you pay your retirement plan back with interest. That is better than paying interest to someone else, but there is a dark side. You are surrendering other earnings your savings would have earned if you did not take it out of the account for the loan. Also, if you change employers or cannot pay back the loan for any reason, you must pay the entire loan back immediately, or you have to pay taxes on the loan balance plus a 10% penalty. That is an outcome that you want to avoid at all costs.

Do not shortchange saving for retirement to fund a business, an extravagant wedding, or to fund your child's education at a costly private school. One of the greatest gifts you can give your children is not to have to rely on them for money when you are older.

If you change jobs, you usually have the option of keeping your retirement savings in your old 401(k), rolling your old 401(k) into your new employer's 401(k) plan, or rolling your old 401(k) into an IRA. I recommend that you roll your old 401(k) into an IRA.

This option will accomplish a couple of good things. First, if you change employers several times during your career, you may end up with five, ten, or more retirement accounts. That is difficult to track and manage. If you transfer all your accounts to one IRA, things are much easier to manage.

Secondly (and more importantly), you get to choose your IRA, and you can select one with extremely low annual fees and a wide array of investment choices. A wisely chosen IRA will have lower annual fees than any 401(k). Excellent options for opening a low-cost IRA include Vanguard, Charles Schwab, and Fidelity Investments. My wife and I have IRAs at Vanguard, and I helped my Mom start one there as well. Good enough for my Mom, good enough for you.

A word of caution is needed here. You should directly transfer your 401(k) into your IRA account. Do *not* have them send the money to you personally and then deposit the check into the IRA. If you get the cash delivered directly to you, it can complicate your taxes. Also, if you make a mistake, you may end up having to pay taxes and penalties on your retirement savings. Do not take that chance. I repeat, have the money transferred directly into your IRA.

The whole idea of saving for your retirement is so that you can enjoy your long, happy retirement. Unfortunately, some of us do not make it to a ripe old age. In any case, when we die, our retirement plan can continue living. In most cases, our beneficiaries can keep the retirement savings in a retirement account for years, or even forever. This feature is an excellent benefit because our beneficiaries can choose to keep the investments in the retirement plan earning money tax-deferred for decades.

Laws will change over time, and the rules for different retirement plans vary. Therefore, it is difficult to give specific advice now that will be good for the long-term future. What we can do is make sure our beneficiaries know that they may have the option to keep the retirement savings earning money tax-deferred. We should emphasize that decisions on the funds they inherit can have a massive impact over the rest of their life, and they should seek financial advice if needed. Finally, we need to keep our retirement plan beneficiaries and our will up to date. It is one last gift we can give to the ones we love.

Investing for the Long-Term

One of the most common mistakes that people make when saving for retirement is to direct their savings into "safe" investments. At first blush, this might be confusing. Shouldn't you want your retirement investments to be safe? The answer is a little counterintuitive. You *don't* want your savings to be safe in the short-term. You *do* want them to be safe for the long-term. These are not the same thing.

In most employer-sponsored retirement plans such as a 401(k) or 403(b), you generally have a choice of a combination of three underlying investment types: stock mutual funds, bond mutual funds, or short-term interest funds. Investment options in other retirement plans are often more varied, but the choices remain very similar: stocks, bonds, or short-term interest investments.

What exactly are these investment choices, and what are their characteristics? A share of common stock represents ownership in a company. So, if you own a share of Apple stock, this means that you own part of Apple incorporated. It is a very tiny part, but you are part owner.

There is another type of stock called preferred stock, which does not represent true ownership of a company. Also, individuals should generally not invest in preferred stock. Typically, if someone uses the word "stock," they are talking about common stock, not preferred stock.

If you own a bond, this means that you have loaned money to a government or company, usually for several years. Hopefully, they will pay you back with interest. If you make a short-term interest investment, you have loaned money to a company, government, or financial institution such as a bank for a year or less. If you have a savings account at a local bank, then you have a short-term interest account.

A mutual fund is a managed portfolio of investments that invest your money in a diversified group of investments of a particular type. The reason that mutual funds are preferred in retirement accounts is that they are safer for the long-term. So, for example, if you invest in the stock of a company and that company goes bankrupt, you will lose your entire investment. That is not safe.

On the other hand, if you invest in a mutual fund that invests in the stocks of all 500 companies in the S&P 500 index, your downside is much more limited. Even if they do, your investment in the other companies should make you enough money to offset those losses. This diversification is the proverbial equivalent of not having all your eggs in one basket. One egg may break, but the rest should be fine.

New financial products come out yearly, and some may be available to you in your retirement plan and elsewhere. Still, they are rarely more than a marginal improvement over existing investment options. On the other hand, they are quite often worse than existing investment choices. Therefore, if you come across an investment that is not mentioned in this book, tread with caution.

Now, back to the common mistake of investing retirement money in something that is too safe. Short-term interest investments are the safest investments. These types of investments go by many names, such as money market funds or guaranteed income funds. They rarely, if ever, go down in value. That sounds great, but the problem is that they earn a low return over the long-term. The reason why you can receive a guaranteed profit is that the return is so low.

Over the long-term, short-term interest investments have historically earned 3% to 4%, depending on the time frame measured. That doesn't sound so bad, but after you factor in inflation, which has historically averaged around 3%, you find that this type of investment has historically just barely surpassed inflation. Therefore, you will earn approximately 1% after inflation. That is a terrible long-term return, and this is why short-term interest investments should be avoided in long-term retirement savings.

Bond mutual funds are a better choice than short-term interest funds for your long-term retirement savings, but they are not the best choice. Historically, bonds have returned about 6% over the long-term. Once again, this depends on the period measured. Additionally, it depends on the type of bond you are measuring. Still, the return of bonds over the long-term should be around 3% higher than inflation.

The best choice for long-term retirement savings is a common stock mutual fund. Over the long-term stocks have returned approximately 9%, depending on the period measured.

So, if over the long-term stocks earn 9%, bonds earn 6%, and short-term interest investments earn 3%, why would anyone invest in the lower returning investments?

The answer is because the lower returning investments are less volatile (or safer) in the short-term. The value of short-term interest investments rarely goes down over a year. Bonds can go down in value as interest rates rise, and they are much more volatile than short-term interest investments.

In contrast, stocks are very volatile over the short-term. For example, the S&P stock index has declined over 20% in value on eleven separate occasions since 1929. Starting in October 2007, the S&P 500 dropped over 56% in the next 17 months. Therefore, stocks are not a suitable investment if you need the money invested returned in less than five years.

This type of short-term volatility is very unnerving to many investors. It can be very unnerving to see your retirement savings go down over 50%. Still, if an investor bailed out of stocks at the bottom of the market in March 2009, they would have missed out on the 300% gain in the S&P 500 over the next nine years.

If you have a stock mutual fund in your retirement account (and you should), it can be tough to ignore short-term losses. Yet, that is exactly what you should do. After all, retirement investments should have a 30 to 50-year time horizon. Still, the steep short-term losses in stocks frighten many investors into less scary investments like bonds and short-term interest investments.

Retirement savings should be long-term, so it is essential to look at long-term historical returns. According to a 2012 Credit Suisse study of long-term returns, stocks returned an average of 9.3% per year, treasury bonds returned 5.0% per year, and short-term interest returns were less than that. I have seen numerous studies of stocks for many long-term periods and have never seen a study that found stocks returned less than 9% yearly. Keeping in mind that there is no guarantee that future returns will match past performance, these studies point out why stocks seem to be the wisest investment for the long-term.

What about the worst long-term returns stocks have ever earned? A 2013 study by Wisdom Tree Asset Management looked at the history of U.S. stocks since 1871. The study found that the worst 30-year period return was 4.2% per year. Please note that this period included the Great Depression. We certainly all want to earn more than 4.2% per year from our stock investments over 30 years. But I find it comforting to know that even during the period that included the Great Depression, stocks had a decent return. Importantly, a 4.2% return is better than the average return that a short-term interest account earns.

Because of the superior historical long-term returns of stocks, I heartily recommend that anyone under the age of 40 invest all of their retirement savings in stock mutual funds, preferably in a total stock market index fund with very low annual fees. Twenty-five years before your planned retirement date, it is okay to start contributing a portion of your retirement savings to a bond mutual fund. Still, I would limit that to 20% of your retirement savings. Once you get to within ten years of your retirement, it is okay to put up to 10% of your retirement funds into short-term interest investments.

Personally, all of my investments in my retirement accounts are in stocks, and I am less than ten years from retirement. I do have a high-risk tolerance, though, and my retirement savings have grown nicely for the over 30 years that I have been saving for retirement.

Keep in mind that the advice in this section is related to long-term savings. If you need money in the next five years, it should not be invested totally in stocks. The rule of thumb is that you should have at least a percentage of your retirement savings in stocks greater than 120 minus your age. For example, if you are 30 years old, 120 minus 30 equals 90. Therefore, according to this rule of thumb, a 30-year-old should have *at least* 90% of their retirement savings in stocks. According to this rule, a 50-year-old should have at least 70% of their retirement savings in stocks.

Some retirement plans give the option of investing retirement savings in the employing company's stock. You should avoid investing a significant portion of your retirement savings in your employer's stock. Investing a lot in just one stock is too risky. If your employer begins having trouble or goes bankrupt, you could lose your job while your investment in the company's stock goes to zero. Please avoid this situation with great vigor.

You may still be thinking that the difference between a 4%, 6%, and 9% return is not a lot, so maybe you should stick with the less volatile investment choices. But, over time, the difference between the performances of these different investments becomes quite large because of the effect of compounded returns.

For example, let's say you are investing $3,000 a year into your retirement account for 45 years. Additionally, let's say that these are the expected yearly returns for your investment options: money market fund (4%), bond fund (6%), and stock fund (9%). In this scenario, the accounts would have the following amounts in them after 45 years: money market fund ($363,088), the bond fund ($638,230), and the stock fund ($1,577,576).

Yikes! That's right, the small percentage difference in return *year after year* becomes quite substantial over time. At the end of 45 years, the stock fund has over four times as much money in it than the "super safe" money market fund and well over twice as much as the safe bond fund.

I believe that evidence strongly supports the decision to have the vast majority of your retirement savings invested in stocks until you get less than twenty years from retirement.

The fear of losing money keeps people from investing. If they do invest, the fear of losing money can keep them from investing in the right thing. Fear of losing money is not unfounded. In the short-term, losses will happen if you invest in any investment that is not risk-free. Still, risky investments have an advantage over risk-free investments. Namely, risky investments generally have a significantly higher return than risk-free investments.

Theoretically, there is only one type of investment that is risk-free. That type of investment is one that is backed fully by the United States of America's Federal Government. These include USA Treasury Bills (also called T-Bills), Treasury Notes, and Treasury Bonds. If you invest in a Treasury security, you are loaning the US government money for less than one year (T-Bill), between one and ten years (T-Note), or greater than ten years (T-Bonds). In each case, the government will pay your money back with interest. Risk-free investments also include those fully backed by a USA Federal Government guarantee such as a Federal Deposit Insurance Corporation (FDIC) guaranteed savings at banks.

As long as the USA government stays intact, these types of investments will be free of risk, but that does not mean they will be suitable investments. An important reason for this is inflation. Inflation is a measure of how fast a dollar loses purchasing power. Inflation can vary substantially from year to year, but it generally runs at an annual rate of 2% - 3%.

Let's say inflation is running at a 3% annual rate. This means that a dollar will buy 3% fewer goods and services a year from now. Now, let's say that you have a risk-free investment earning a 2% rate of return during this year. Then your investment is earning less than the inflation rate, thus lowering your purchasing power. So, even though your investment earned a return, you lost purchasing power. In general, we would prefer that our investments make a return that is higher than inflation. Therefore, even though an investment may be technically risk-free, it does incur the risk of not keeping up with inflation.

Historically, risk-free investments have earned returns slightly higher than inflation before taxes. After taxes, they often haven't kept up with inflation. On the other hand, wisely chosen risky investments such as stocks and corporate bonds have historically had returns well above inflation, even after taxes.

So, risk-free sounds excellent, and it is a beautiful thing if you are investing for the short-term. But, if you are investing for decades, you should take some risks. Evidence strongly suggests that investing in stocks and corporate bonds for the long-term ensures more substantial retirement savings than if you invest the majority of your money in risk-free investments.

No one knows what inflation will be in the future. Also, no one knows what the return of short-term safe investments such as money markets will be in the future. Finally, we don't know what the yields on stocks and corporate bonds will be in the future. As you can deduce, this makes it hard to plan for the future.

These murky future scenarios don't mean that we shouldn't plan for the future. These uncertainties mean that we should put more effort into preparing for the future. So, should we throw up our hands and cry to the heavens? No, we should make decisions based on what has happened in the past and what is likely to occur in the future.

We can use assumptions that we used earlier based on historical facts to evaluate future long-term investment options. Let's assume that in the future, long-term stocks earn 9%, corporate bonds earn 6%, and money market investments make 4%. There is no guarantee that these predicted returns will be accurate. But there are compelling fundamental economic reasons that stock returns will be higher than corporate bond returns over the long-term. Similarly, the long-term returns of bonds should exceed short-term interest rates. Therefore, even if our projections are not accurate, they should provide a framework for making profitable long-term investment decisions.

To make things simple, let's assume that we are saving $1,000 a year until retirement and retiring at age 70. In reality, you may retire at a different age and put way more money into your retirement account each year. Hopefully, you will not put in less. Also, the amount you put into retirement will vary from year to year for most people. But these simple assumptions will help to demonstrate some principles.

Let's start with an example where you are doing everything right. You are investing in the riskier investment (stocks) and earning 9% on average per year. You also begin investing for your retirement at 25 years old. Additionally, you are putting your money in a tax-deferred retirement account such as an IRA. After you invest your money in an IRA, it will not be taxed until you take it out in retirement.

In this ideal scenario, your money grows tax-deferred for 45 years until you retire at age 70. In this case, you will have $526,000 (rounded to the nearest thousand dollars) in your retirement account. What if you chose the "safer" investment options in this same scenario? If you invested in bonds (6% return) or a money market fund (4% return), you would have $213,000 or $121,000, respectively. Wow! That is a lot less than $526,000. "Safe" investments are not so safe over the long-term.

It is essential to invest your long-term retirement savings in a tax-deferred account such as an IRA. Let's say you invested the same $1,000 a year in stocks that returned 9% a year, but that you invested it in a taxable account, and you were in the 20% tax bracket. In this case, you would pay taxes on any dividends or capital gains your account earned when you earned them. You would not have $526,000 in your account at age 70, but $303,000. True, you could withdraw original principle from that $303,000 tax-free after retirement, but at a high cost in retirement savings amount.

Let's say you make another common mistake; you don't start saving early enough. Let's say you wait until you are 40 to start saving in an IRA earning 9%. In this case, you only have $136,000 at retirement. Waiting too long to start saving for retirement is a huge error. You would have about one-fourth of the money that you would have if you had started saving at 25.

These examples demonstrate that it is best to start investing early for retirement, invest mostly in stocks, and invest in tax-deferred retirement accounts. You want the 70-year old version of yourself to love your young self, not shout curses at young you.

Inflation is a decrease in the purchasing power of a dollar as prices rise. You may have noticed that prices of commonly purchased items tend to increase over time. Sure, sometimes there are sales or short-term periods where the costs of certain items go down, but generally, prices go up.

Many items, like a US first-class postage stamp, go up in price sometimes, but rarely if ever, go down. The cost of a stamp has risen from 10 cents in 1974 to 50 cents in 2018. Similarly, I can remember buying a full-sized Hershey Chocolate Bar for 5 cents when I was a wee child (yeah, I'm old). Now, one often costs a dollar or more.

Other items, such as gasoline, generally go up over time, but the year-to-year price can fluctuate wildly. The average retail gasoline price rose from 53 cents in 1974 to $3.37 in 2014. But, as any long-time purchaser of gasoline knows, the price is quite volatile over short periods. For example, gas went from $3.61 to $2.58 to $3.02 from 2008 till 2010. Still, the price rises over long periods.

Other items go down in price over time because of improvements in technology or manufacturing processes. Many electronic products have seen this effect. Calculators, PCs, televisions, and cell phones have all seen this effect, at least in their early years of production. I bought a state-of-the-art TV in the 1980s for $500. Recently, I bought a more reliable television with a larger, better-defined picture and a multitude of other improvements for $300. This example of something going down in price is rare, but it does occur.

The overall price increases are a result of inflation. Overall inflation in the USA usually averages around 2-3% per year. It is rarely negative because overall prices rarely decline. There have been periods in the USA when inflation was quite high and painful. Between 1973 and 1981, yearly price inflation exceeded 10% in four years and did not fall below 5% in any year.

That resulted in a substantial decrease in the purchasing power of the dollar. Simply put, people couldn't buy as many of the things they wanted or needed.

Remember when you are calculating how much you will have saved in the future for retirement, that this amount will not account for how inflation reduces the value of money over time. For example, $1,000 in 2018 would only have the purchasing power of $175 in 1973 (45 years earlier). So, if you think that having a million dollars will be a massive amount of savings 45 years from now, don't be so sure. It could be only worth $175,000 or so in today's dollars.

Since inflation can have such a significant effect on the future purchasing price of our savings, we should consider its impact on our rate of return from investments. The impact of inflation on investments and savings can be measured by considering the real rate of return of an investment. The real rate of return is the annual percentage return on an investment after adjusting for inflation (or, in rare cases, deflation). The real rate of return is more important than the actual rate of return (also called the nominal rate of return).

To create an example to explain the real rate of return, let's reuse our assumption about returns for stocks (9%), corporate bonds (6%), and money market investments (4%). Let's also assume a 3% inflation rate. These are realistic assumptions in most years.

The simple formula for estimating a real rate of return is to subtract the inflation rate from the actual rate of return. There is a more precise formula for the real rate of return, but this estimation is quite accurate and suitable for our purposes.

In this scenario, the real rate of return is 6% for stocks, 3% for bonds, and 1% for a money market investment. The use of real rates of return highlights the superiority of higher returning investments when inflation is factored into the equation. In our realistic example, stocks have a real rate of return that is twice as high as bonds and six times that of the money market investment. Remember that the real rate of return is the most important measure of how fast the purchasing power of our long-term investments will grow.

The difference in real rates of return grows even more once taxes are taken into account. If you were invested in the money market fund in a taxable account and you were in the 25% tax bracket, your real after-tax rate of return would 0%. That's right, nada! The reason the already meager real rate of return for the money market investment is wiped out is because you are taxed on the actual rate of return, which is higher than the real rate of return.

The safe return of the money market can be erased by inflation and taxes. "Safe" investments that garner lower yields can be disastrous for long-term wealth creation.

In this case, the real after-tax rate of returns would be 3.75% for stocks and 1.5% for bonds. This example demonstrates the importance of investing in higher returning investments for the long-term and the advantage of having those funds in a tax-deferred retirement account.

If we look at the facts, investing in stocks for the long-term is a no-brainer. On the other hand, in the short-term (and by short, I mean a five-year period or less), investing in stocks can be terrifying. After all, the S&P 500 stock index has declined over 20% in value on eleven separate occasions since 1929, including a 56% loss starting in 2007.

That is why it is a good idea not to obsess over your short-term returns for your retirement investments. If your investments are going down quickly, you may panic and sell your stocks at precisely the wrong time. The mantra is "buy low, sell high," not "buy high, and panic sell low." Still, many people will panic and sell when their investments have gone down considerably in value, the exact worst time to sell. It is funny that people instinctively know to not sell their house just because it has gone down in value because of short-term market conditions. But they often do not understand that about stocks.

Remember, that if you own a widely-diversified portfolio of stocks or stock mutual fund, you own a tiny portion of many great businesses. So, what are the chances that if you own a small part of McDonald's, Exxon, Coca-Cola, Amazon, Apple, Microsoft, Ford, Boeing, Marriott, and Johnson & Johnson that your ownership in these businesses will go down over a long period (over ten years)? The answer is almost nil. The great investor and CEO Warren Buffett recently wrote to Berkshire Hathaway shareholders, "American business -- and consequently a basket of stocks -- is virtually certain to be worth far more in the years ahead."

Good businesses make money most of the time. Even if one or two of these businesses eventually go bankrupt, the other companies will likely make up more than enough money to offset those problems. Since 1871, the worst annual return in U.S. stocks over 30 years was over 4% (a period that included the Great Depression of the 1930s). The median 30-year return since 1871 is well over 9%. The risk of investing in stocks over the long-term exists, but if the worst 30-year performance over the last 150 years is over 4%, how bad is the risk in investing in stocks over the long-term?

If you want to understand long-term investments and retirement planning, and you are willing to put considerable effort into understanding investing, I suggest that you join the American Association of Individual Investors (AAII). The website is aaii.com. As I write this, a one-year membership is $49 a year. I am a lifetime member. If I have a complaint about AAII, it is that they provide too much information. My complaint might be "praising with faint damnation." They call themselves a "nonprofit educational publisher." I agree with this assessment.

AAII will try to sell you additional research, publications, seminars, and conferences. These products are generally quality products at a reasonable price. I haven't purchased anything beyond the website access, and monthly issues of the *AAII Journal* provided free with membership, but I almost certainly will in the future. Again, membership in AAII only makes sense for individuals that want to put in considerable time and effort into understanding investments and retirement planning.

Most people are risk-averse when it comes to their investments; being risk-averse means that we would prefer a guaranteed return over a risky one that had the same average return. For example, given the option of a guaranteed 10% return versus a 50-50 chance at either a 20% return or a 0% return (for an average return of 10%), most people will prefer the sure thing return of 10%.

Risk aversion is normal, and it is a good thing. People that are not risk-averse may even have a gambling problem. Keep in mind that risk aversion does not mean a person will not take any risk. It means that you want to be compensated with an additional *expected* return for taking on risk.

So, for example, a risk-averse person might take a 50-50 chance at either a 30% return or a 0% return (for an average return of 15%) over a guaranteed return of 10%. It just depends if the extra expected return of 15% versus the guaranteed return of 10% is enough compensation to motivate the investor to take the risk.

In general, riskier investments have higher expected returns than safe investments. They have to offer a higher expected return to attract risk-averse investors. That is why stocks have a higher average return than corporate bonds, which have a higher average return than a bank savings account. Stocks have more risk than corporate bonds, which have more risk than the savings account.

This higher risk is why investors should avoid having too much of their investment savings in one or just a few stocks or corporate bonds. The likelihood that a company goes bankrupt and the stock or bond becomes worthless is too high for most rational investors. On the other hand, a diversified portfolio of stocks will almost certainly earn more than a diversified portfolio of corporate bonds. The bonds will almost certainly make more than a savings account in the *long-term*.

Different people have different levels of risk aversion. Everyone should shun risk in their emergency savings and money invested for the short-term. If you need a down payment on a home in two years and your money is invested in stocks, the stock market may go down 50%, and you will need to keep renting.

Researchers have demonstrated that most people experience more pain from losing money than the joy they experience when they make money. Another way to put this is that, for most people, finding $100 does not bring as much pleasure as the pain of losing $100 causes. This behavior is normal, but often not 100% rational. Don't let the fear of losing money cause you to avoid quality investments or sell your long-term investments in a panic.

At some point, someone will try to sell you an annuity. The salesperson will likely have a convincing pitch. Annuities have many variations. The basic idea is that you purchase an annuity from an insurance company or other financial institution, and then you receive guaranteed monthly income for twenty or more years in retirement. Guaranteed income in retirement? Sign me up! No, on second thought, run, run very fast!

Famed investment advisor Ken Fisher has said in a prominent advertisement for his firm, "We don't sell annuities. I would die and go to hell before I would sell an annuity." Yikes! I believe that almost all annuities are terrible investments, but it appears I like them better than Mr. Fisher.

In his commercial and his writings, Fisher goes on to explain some of the reasons that he hates annuities. He has admitted that some fixed annuities are merely okay, but shouldn't we aim for better than just okay in our investment decisions.

Annuity contracts are almost always huge and contain confusing legalese. Generally, you don't know what you are purchasing. Furthermore, the salesperson probably doesn't understand what they are selling you. They know they are getting a huge commission. It is not unusual for the salesperson to make more off of your investment than you do. Yuck!

Annuity purchasers often believe they are getting a guaranteed rate of return when they are merely getting their invested money returned according to a schedule. Any actual guaranteed return you get is sure to be a meager return. If you purchase an annuity and decide you want out of it, you will most likely have to pay a sizeable surrender charge.

Before we got married, my wife was sold an annuity by a representative of a large, reputable bank through a program at the public school system where she worked. This was a variable annuity that was supposed to earn a higher return if the stock market did well. The annuity had made approximately 1% per year over a period when the stock market had done quite well. Outrageous! This investment had been sold to my wife as a retirement investment when she was in her twenties, and it was earning 1% per year. I guarantee you the salesman made a lot more money than my wife.

I decided she should sell the annuity and invest the proceeds in an IRA. The annuity was worth $1,300, and she had to pay a $300 surrender charge to get out of this bummer of an investment. After the surrender charge, only $1,000 remained. Still, I preferred to have $1,000 earning 8% or so annually in the stock market over having $1,300 making 1% for the next 30+ years. Thank goodness she had not invested her life savings in the annuity, as so many people do.

Annuities can include tax-deferred earnings, a death benefit, variable payments that can go up, and a myriad of other clauses. But the bottom line is that most of them are terrible investments. Also, annuities are guaranteed income, but what if the financial institution that guarantees the investment goes out of business? In this case, you could lose your entire investment.

Don't let the promise of guaranteed income cloud your judgment. I strongly advise you to avoid annuities even if they are sold to you by what appears to be a knowledgeable and friendly person from an extremely reputable financial firm. Of course, they will tell you that their annuities are the exception and they are great investments. Please, just say no.

Make Regular Investing a Habit Today. Yes, Today!

One effective way to reduce risk and increase average investment return is to dollar-cost average. Dollar-cost averaging involves investing the same amount of money every period, usually every month, in the same investment(s). By default, Employer retirement plans such as a 401(k) or a 403(b) use dollar-cost averaging.

The advantage of dollar-cost averaging is that it will lower your average purchase price of the investment, thus increasing our return. Let's look at an example. I am going to use round numbers that are a little extreme to demonstrate dollar-cost averaging, but the math will give a similar result for more realistic investing scenarios.

Let's say you want to invest $2,400 in a stock that is currently $100 a share. You can invest immediately, and you will buy 24 shares. Another alternative is to dollar-cost average your investment over the next few years, investing $600 at the start of each year.

Let's say the price of the stock fluctuates (as stocks are wont to do). The price is $100 today, $150 a year from now, $50 two years from now, and back to $100 three years from now. If we invested all of our money at the start at $100 a share, we are back to break-even because the stock price three years from now is back at $100.

What if we invested $600 each of the four years for a total of $2,400? Today, our $600 would buy us 6 shares. The next year, we could buy 4 shares at $150 a share. After that, we would buy 12 shares at $50 a share. Finally, we would buy another 6 shares at $100.

Now, we have invested the same $2,400 using dollar-cost averaging at $600 a year. Without dollar-cost averaging, we bought 24 shares. With dollar-cost averaging, we purchased six shares, then four shares, then 12 shares, then six shares for a total of 28 shares.

It's a miracle! Without dollar-cost averaging, we bought 24 shares with our $2,400. With dollar-cost averaging, we purchased 28 shares with the same amount of money. How can this be?

Dollar-cost averaging works because we are investing the same amount of money every period. We buy more shares when the price is low and fewer shares when the price is high. This lowers our average purchase price. A lower price is better. "Buy low, sell high" is an investment cliché for a reason. It is sound advice.

Dollar-cost averaging is an excellent way to invest. It takes discipline, but investing at regular intervals is an excellent investment strategy. As we have demonstrated here, dollar-cost averaging tends to lower your purchase price for your investments.

There is an exception to the advantage of dollar-cost averaging. If the investment soars straight up and continues rising, you would be better off investing the full amount from day one.

But, this type of investment is the exception, not the rule. Resist the urge to practice market timing, selling when you think prices are high and buying when you think they are low. Market timing is extremely difficult, and even most financial professionals that try it perform worse than if they had just kept their money invested.

Most investments fluctuate a great deal over time. Dollar-cost average investing is a way to take advantage of these fluctuations to "buy low."

There is a huge advantage to starting your retirement savings when you are young. If you start young, you can take advantage of the power of compound returns. Compound returns is similar to compound interest. Compound interest is when you not only earn interest on your original deposit, but you also begin to earn interest on interest. Over time, you will start to make more interest on interest than the interest you are earning on your original deposit.

With compound returns, you not only earn money on your original investment but on your earlier returns from the investment. Like compound interest, your returns from your previous returns grow exponentially with time. Furthermore, because of the strong effect of cumulative returns, a small difference in annual returns can grow into a massive difference over time. Let's demonstrate these concepts.

First, let's look at two people that have waited until they are 40 years old to start saving for retirement. Let's assume they plan to invest in a well-diversified portfolio that will earn 7% per year. One decides to save $2,000 a year for the next 30 years, and the other decides to save $3,000 a year. When these two people retire at 70 years old, the first person will have $189,000 in savings, and the second person will have $283,000.

Now, let's look at two people that start saving at 25 years old in a portfolio that also earns 7% annually, one saving $2,000 a year and the other $3,000 a year. If these two individuals retire at 70, the former individual will have $571,000, and the latter will have $857,000.

It is evident that the investors that invested $3,000 per year will have more money than the investors that invested $2,000 per year at retirement. It is less apparent that the investors that started earlier will do much better.

Let's recap. The late investors that invested for 30 years had $189,000 ($2,000 per year) and $283,000 ($3,000 per year) at retirement. The investors that started early and invested for 45 years had $571,000 ($2,000 per year) and $857,000 ($3,000 per year) at retirement.

Investing $2,000 per year beginning at age 25 resulted in $571,000 at retirement. Investing $3,000 per year beginning at age 40 resulted in $283,000 at retirement. These results highlight the fact that it is better to start saving for retirement early, even if you are saving less money.

I want to emphasize that you should start saving for retirement immediately, even if you are starting at a late age. In this case, better late than never definitely holds. Please, do not use past failures to save as an excuse not to start saving today. After all, have you ever heard anyone complain that they had too much money saved for retirement?

Chapter 8: Avoid Investing Mistakes

Stay Calm and Invest Rationally (It's Not Easy)

When I was in my early thirties, my girlfriend at the time announced that she wanted to spend a weekend at the casinos on the Mississippi Gulf Coast. She had never been to a casino and thought it would be fun. I had never been to a casino either and didn't have a strong desire to go, but I figured that we would at least be on the beach, and she was really cute.

She had an affinity for the slots. I decided that I would just bet $50 on one number for one spin of the roulette wheel and then gamble no more. I would have a one out of 39 chance at winning, but if I won, I would earn $1,750. I didn't enjoy gambling, but I thought this would be a thrilling moment. Furthermore, I would have a good story forever, especially if I hit on my less than 3% chance of winning. In any case, I would only spend a few moments in the casino. Then, I could spend the rest of the weekend, having fun doing beach stuff alone until my girlfriend ran out of quarters.

The night before we went to the casino, my girlfriend dreamed I put the $50 on 13 red and won. I decided that I would put the bet on 13 because if it came up, I did not want to say I went against her premonition.

After she sat down to start her session with the one-armed bandits, I decided to go over to the roulette table to put my bet down. Then, I wimped. I decided that instead of putting the whole $50 on one spin, I would put $10 down per turn until I won or lost the $50. If I hit, I would only earn $350, but that would pay for the weekend (remember, this was in the early nineties).

I wanted to make sure I understood how to play the game and when to put bets down. I didn't want to make a mistake that would result in a run-in with one of the sturdy security guards putting a hurting on me. Therefore, I quietly watched for about 15 minutes nearby before I stepped up to the table.

I put my $10 chip down on 13 black (not red). I already knew that the dream was not 100% accurate because 13 is always black. I won on the first spin, stuck to my plan, raked in my $350, and cashed in all my chips. At the time, if you won that much money in that casino, they had a guard escort you to collect your winnings. Therefore, I had to wait by the table for a few minutes.

During that time, several of the people that had been playing while I studied the table and while I won decided that I must have some sort of system. They were convinced I had a special skill or knowledge. In retrospect, it must have looked odd. It appeared I had studied the spins for 15 minutes and then stepped up and knew exactly what number to bet.

I knew nothing. Unlike poker, blackjack, and sports betting, roulette is 100% luck. That is why I chose to play it. I knew the odds were against me like they are in all casino games, but I knew I had as good a chance as anyone else. It was pure luck.

My girlfriend gave me grief about not betting the full $50, but I still got a good story and a paid-for weekend. I haven't gambled in a casino since then, and I don't intend to bet in the future. I plan on dying as one of the very few people that won more at a casino than he lost.

The other bettors' belief that I must have had some particular skill illustrated a great truth about investing. Frequently, luck is mistaken for expertise or knowledge. Many beginning investors make a killing on a few investments early on and become convinced that it is because they are very skillful. They become assured they can keep on picking outstanding investments. "Never mind all the advice of all those seasoned experts, they don't know what I know."

Then reality hits. The winners become losers, and they stop investing. If I had kept at the roulette wheel, I would have eventually lost everything. I didn't have the skill, just early luck even though the odds were against me.

This roulette example illustrates how luck can be confused with skill and that this confusion should be avoided while investing. It is important to note that there is a considerable difference between betting in a casino and investing in the stock market. The bettors, on average, lose money. Investors, on average, earn money. In both cases, luck should never be confused with skill and knowledge.

There is one area in which gamblers and investors often behave similarly. Both tend to remember their winners and brag about them. They both also tend to forget their losers and don't necessarily learn from these mistakes.

Have you ever heard a person purchasing a scratch-off lottery ticket talk about the time that they or a friend of theirs won $100 or $500? I have on several occasions. Have you ever heard someone purchasing a scratch-off talk about the hundreds or thousands of losing tickets that they have purchased? Me, neither. But most people that buy scratch-offs regularly have lost hundreds of times or more.

This illustrates an important point. The evidence of returns on our investments should not be anecdotal. Hard evidence of returns over long periods is useful. Anecdotal evidence is not.

If I purchase a $2 scratch-off and win $500, that does not provide evidence that I should invest my life savings in scratch-off tickets. That would be insane. Similarly, if I invest in a penny stock or cyber currency and make a considerable return, that is not sufficient evidence to indicate that I should do it again.

Historically, a widely-diversified stock portfolio or stock mutual fund has earned an average annual return of around 8% - 10% for the long-term. Some have made some valid arguments why these returns could be marginally lower in the next twenty years. Indeed, these returns can be very negative for periods of less than five years. Still, the hard evidence suggests that stocks are an excellent investment over the long-term.

Often, when one group of people is thriving in an investment for the short-term, other investors pile into similar investments quickly. In this scenario, the price of investments can promptly become divorced from the actual value of the investments. Prices rise quickly on the hope that someone else will buy your stake from you at an amount higher than you paid for it. This is called a bubble, and it is based on the Greater Fool Theory. This theory suggests that it does not matter if you foolishly paid too much for an asset as long as you can get a "Greater Fool" to pay more for it.

Bubbles can go on for quite some time. Still, if the price of assets is much higher than the actual value, the bubble is bound to burst, and prices will collapse. Examples of financial bubbles go at least as far back as the tulip mania in the 17th century in Holland. Tulip prices (yes, tulips) kept going up as more and more people purchased them for ever-higher prices until the cost of one bulb of particularly desirable tulips were going for the price of a house. It did not end well. After a few years, the price of a tulip fell to, well, what a tulip should be worth.

More recent examples of extreme bubbles in the USA are available. In 2001, the stock value of nascent internet companies with no revenue, no profits, and minimal assets were selling for billions of dollars. Within a few years, many of these companies were bankrupt, and their investors lost everything. In 2008, many homes were selling for twice or more of the actual value of the house. These mispricings ended in the financial crisis, which caused extreme financial distress to millions of Americans.

There will be more bubbles. There will probably be times when you hear that you are a fool if you do not invest in something that is going up in value at an incredible rate. Don't believe it. Don't be the greater fool.

Warren Buffett, perhaps the most successful investor of all time, states that rule number 1 of money is "never lose money." His second rule of investing is "don't forget rule number 1." Yet, even Buffett has lost money on some of his investments, but not many. Still, Buffett's rules point out a successful strategy for getting better than average returns on your investments. Namely, avoid investments that are likely to earn sub-standard returns or lose money. John Bogle, the founder of Vanguard and pioneer of index investing, put it well, "successful investing involves doing a few things right and avoiding serious mistakes." Let's look at some mistakes that should be avoided.

If an investment that sounds too good to be true, it probably is, and it should be avoided. Any investment promising high returns with little or no risk is not to be trusted. Conversely, if someone tells you that an investment has the potential for extremely high returns, but it is very risky, and you might lose everything, they may be telling you the truth. In general, stay away from investments that you do not understand.

Don't follow unsolicited investment advice, especially via email. It is highly likely that this advice will be high-cost subpar advice at best and a scam at worst. You will see advertisements touting successful investors that have made fortunes in very little time with small investments. These advertisements are either wholly false or majorly misleading. The investor could have lucked into the upside of an asset bubble, and they want you to get into the downside of it.

Others are the equivalent of lottery winners claiming they can help you to win the next lottery. They were just lucky, and they can't recreate that luck. An investor could have become very rich by investing all of their money in Microsoft, Amazon, or Starbucks during the early years. But it is extremely difficult to pick the next super stock.

Don't Invest in Sketchy Stuff

Many of my undergraduate students, especially males, have expressed an interest in penny stocks. Penny stocks are generally defined as stocks that sell for $3 to $5 or less. Many of them literally sell for pennies a share. I always advise my students to avoid penny stocks. I also advise against buying Over the Counter (OTC) stocks and stocks listed in the pink sheets. Some of my students ignore this advice.

I can see the attraction to penny stocks. The student only has a few hundred dollars to invest, and they want to make some real money fast from their investment. Sure, they could invest in a reliable company like Exxon or Starbucks and likely earn an 8% return or so over the long-term, but there is no patience for this.

They have read or heard about someone paying a few cents a share for stock in some company that soon shoots up in value to $10 a share or more for a thousand percent plus return in just a few years. That is the kind of return they want, and the truth is that similar outlandish performances have occurred previously. Still, the truth is many more people lose most or all of their money in penny stocks, and only a few earn positive returns. The few extraordinary stories of high returns end up in advertisements, and the losers do not.

The truth is that many penny stocks are shell companies with little or no assets, revenue, or earnings. It is legal for a person to sell stock in a company with no assets, sales, or profits with only an idea. Then, the person can pay themselves an excellent salary while they try and fail to implement the concept. The company goes broke, but the person that sold the stock walks away with all the money.

The penny stock company may be based on a solid idea. Against my advice, some of my students invested in penny stocks that were planning to sell marijuana in Colorado immediately after it became legal to do so. At first, the price of the stocks soared, and my students were looking pretty smart. After all, there was little doubt that recreational marijuana in Colorado was going to become a billion-dollar business soon.

The recreational marijuana industry in Colorado has prospered, but the companies that my students invested in did not participate profitably. My students' investments soared and then tanked. They lost a lot of money.

There are some legitimate companies with realistic chances of success that are traded as penny stocks, OTC, or in the Pink Sheets. On the other hand, the number of companies traded in these areas that go bankrupt or lose investors' money is quite high. These investments are very risky.

The reasons that these types of investments are risky are numerous. First, many have little or no assets or revenue. In my opinion, that is not a company; it is an idea. Secondly, the bid-ask spread for these types of investments is often huge.

The bid price of a stock is the price at which a broker is willing to buy a stock. The ask price is the price at which a broker is ready to sell a stock. For the stock of major corporations such as McDonald's, the difference between this bid price and ask price (the bid-ask spread) is usually a penny or two.

The bid-ask spread is usually much higher for penny, OTC, and Pink Sheets stocks. It is not unusual for the spread to be 30% of the price of the stock or more. What does this mean? Let's say you buy a stock that has a bid price of $1.00 and an ask price of $1.50. You decide to buy 1000 shares. You will need to invest $1,500 for the 1,000 shares at the ask price of $1.50. If you immediately decide you want to sell the shares, you will not get your $1,500 back. You will only get $1,000 because you can only sell at the bid price of $1.00. You have lost 1/3 of your money simply due to the bid-ask spread.

Another disadvantage of buying stocks that are not trading on the New York Stock Exchange or the NASDAQ exchange is that these exchanges have financial stability standards. They verify that the companies listed on their exchanges are legitimate companies that meet specific criteria. This extra vetting is a valuable benefit to the investor. It is not a guarantee that the company will not go bankrupt or commit fraud, but it is a significant protection against the probability of these occurrences. I strongly advise against investing in penny stocks, and stocks that trade OTC or in the Pink Sheets.

When I was a graduate finance student, I attended a question and answer session with Warren Buffett. It was an enlightening experience. One thing that still stands out in my mind about that event was Buffett's answer to a question about shorting a stock. Shorting is a method used to benefit financially when the price of a stock goes down.

Buffett replied that he often knew of a stock that appeared way overpriced and that he was confident that the stock price would go down. He had shorted stocks before, but he had decided that he never wanted to short a stock again. He reasoned that stocks could stay irrationally overpriced for longer than you could afford the money to short the stock. I decided that I would never short a stock, and I have never shorted one. I urge you to do the same.

If you choose to become exceptionally informed on investing, you will come across the concept of buying stocks or other investments on margin. "Margin" is a fancy way to say borrow some money to invest. The idea is simple, borrow at a lower rate and earn a higher rate of return. It is a lucrative system if it works that way. The problem is that it often doesn't. Let's say you are borrowing money at a 6% rate to buy stocks on margin, hoping for a 10% return. If stock prices go up, you are golden. If stock prices decline, especially if they drop by a lot, you are likely to lose most of your investment. If stock prices go down enough, you get a margin call. That means that you have to sell the stocks you bought on margin, whether you want to or not. Do not buy on margin.

If you buy a call or put option, you get the right to buy (call) or sell (put) a stock at a pre-specified price for a specified period in the future. Options can be used in conjunction with stock ownership by sophisticated investors to reduce risk. Options purchased alone by unsophisticated investors are one of the riskiest investments available. It is very common for an option purchase to result in a 100% loss.

Investing in commodities and futures is also not advisable. Commodities include metals such as gold, silver, and copper; grains such as corn, wheat, and soybeans; meat such as hogs, pork bellies (bacon), and cattle, and energy such as oil and natural gas. Futures are agreements to buy or sell these commodities or other assets at a future date at a specified price.

In general, the purchase or sale of a commodity or future is a zero-sum transaction. In a zero-sum game, every dollar that one party makes in the deal is offset by a dollar loss for the other party. In other words, the overall gain of both parties is zero. It is worse, though, because, after commissions and fees, the average return is a loss.

If you invest in commodities and futures, the opposite party in your transaction is likely to be a bright individual working for a sophisticated investment company with a supercomputer and the latest information. Still, want to play? I don't.

These Investments Sound Good, But History Says "Not So Much"

Gold has been considered a reliable investment for centuries. Historically though, gold has rarely been a particularly lucrative long-term investment. If you purchase gold, you will have to pay to store it and insure it. Alternatively, you can keep it in your home and risk losing it.

Gold does tend to have occasional runs where it is a good investment for a few years. When this happens, rest assured you will see commercials, advertisements, and experts on TV informing you that you are a fool if you do not invest in gold. Usually, investing in gold after it has had a good run is the worst time to do so.

Some investment experts advise having 5% or so of your portfolio in gold in case there is an apocalypse. There is only a little harm in following this advice, but I would rather have ammunition and emergency foodstuffs in such a scenario.

Warren Buffett offered a concise explanation of why he considered gold to be a sub-par investment in Berkshire Hathaway's 2011 annual report (produced in 2012). He categorized gold as an asset that did not provide anything except the hope that someone else will pay more for it in the future.

He noted that "if you own one ounce of gold for an eternity, you will still own one ounce at its end." At the time, Buffett noted that recent bubbles in internet stocks and houses had not ended well. Investors had been willing to pay more until they didn't. Then, the bubble burst.

When Buffett warned of a potential gold bubble in the 2011 annual report, gold was trading for $1,750 per ounce. In 2018, gold sold for $1,250 an ounce. Those that ignored Buffett's advice in 2011 got about a -30% return on their investment over six years. Score one for the Oracle of Omaha.

Over the long-term, an investment in gold has basically matched the rate of inflation. But, with storage and insurance costs, gold has an even lower return. Over the long-term, stocks and bonds have handily beaten inflation with no need for insurance or storage costs. I would follow Buffett's advice and avoid investing in gold. My only investment in gold is my wife's and my wedding rings. At least, that has proved to be an excellent investment in gold for the long-term.

In the 1980s, an amateur violinist spent $700,000 for two rare and exquisite violins. Twenty-five years later, the violins were worth $13,000,000, and the owner had collected an additional $750,000 for allowing virtuosos to play his violins. The return on his investment appears astounding. In fact, the return is over 1,860%. Additionally, the owner gets to interact with some of the best conductors and musicians in the world. Also, he enjoys showing his treasures off.

Why would anyone invest in anything other than rare and collectible investments like the violins? It turns out that there are some excellent reasons. First of all, when you look at long-term returns, they appear to be much higher than they are because of compounding. The astounding 1,860% return turns out to be a more reasonable, though still quite good, return of 13% per year. Of course, not all collectibles or rare assets have a return this high. Also, if you add in maintenance, storage, and insurance costs, the annual return on the violins and most collectibles would be reduced considerably.

Additionally, there are often sales commissions involved in buying and selling collectibles. There is usually a large bid-ask spread. So, for example, if you buy a comic book at the local shop for $25 and return to sell it back in a month, they may only give you $12 for it. If you see a price quoted for a collectible, that is usually the price you can buy it at (the ask price). But if you go to sell the item, you will receive the lower bid price.

If you are buying primarily to profit from your investment, you will probably be competing with experts that are also trying to make money on their investments. Therefore, you better be an expert to have a chance of earning favorable returns.

Another problem is that collectibles don't always go up in value. Many can soar for a while, then stagnate, and then eventually decline, sometimes to the point that they have little or no value. A 2016 article from TheStreet.com, "10 Worthless Collectibles and the Reasons They Lost Their Value", declared that many *investments* that were once valuable had declined precipitously to the point that they had very little value. These formerly valuable items included Coca-Cola memorabilia, Americana, Roseville pottery, Thomas Kinkade paintings, Hummel figurines, comic books, commemorative plates, baseball cards, Beanie Babies, and lunch boxes. Many stamps and coins have lost value also as collectors have lost interest. In the 1950s, collecting these types of items constituted fun. Now, many people would prefer to use social media or play video games for entertainment.

I had often watched the PBS show "Antiques Roadshow" when a person was amazed at how much an item they owned had gone up in value over decades. Ever the downer, I do the math and realize that their fantastic returns are often actually low single-digit annual percentage returns. A small profit is okay if you enjoy owning the item, but it should not be considered a substantial investment.

To demonstrate how long-term returns can appear more extraordinary than they are, let's take a look at the performance of the S&P 500 stock index with reinvested dividends. These returns are very similar to what you could get by investing in a low-fee S&P index mutual fund. An investment $1,000 in June of 1978 would have been worth over $83,000 forty years later. This return is over 8,200%. It appears to be an astonishing return, but the annual return is more pedestrian.

The performance works out to an 11.7% annual return. That is a healthy return that I would be happy to get on my retirement savings, but it is not incredible. It is merely an average return for stock investments for the period. This example demonstrates a couple of concepts. First, performances that appear to be extraordinary over the long-term can be revealed as ordinary returns once the annual return is calculated. Secondly, the average return of investing in stocks tends to be quite good over the long-term.

I have noticed that the returns of collectibles and rare items are often quoted as to how they went from one value to another over a very long period. This method tends to make the returns appear much more spectacular than they are. Keep this in mind when you are considering investing in collectibles or other investments, especially if you are impressed by seemingly impressive long-term returns. Always calculate the annual percentage return to get a more accurate picture of the investment return, and don't forget the insurance, storage, and maintenance.

I have an otherwise normal friend that enjoyed collecting toy trains. He went to conventions and would buy and sell train sets and earn enough money to pay for his travel costs. Therefore, he broke even on his mini-business. But, he enjoyed the conventions and setting up the trains in his basement and playing with them and showing them to friends. Therefore, he got enjoyment and what amounted to free vacations from his investment in his trains. If you can break even doing that, I'd say it is a worthwhile endeavor.

He eventually decided to liquidate his train collection. I believe his beautiful wife had a little to do with this decision. He had simply found other things that he enjoyed more.

I advise you to buy collectibles if you enjoy having them and you can afford them. I don't recommend you to view them as suitable investments, even if they may work out that way if you are fortunate or are an expert in the field.

Collectibles don't pay interest or dividends to you. Conversely, they usually cost you because of insurance, maintenance, and storage. That is why I advise you to view them as entertainment with a possible investment kicker and not as a significant part of your investment portfolio.

Chapter 9 – Investing in Stocks

Most People Shouldn't Invest in Individual Stocks

You can be a very successful investor without ever investing in individual stocks. My advice for most people is to forgo investing in individual stocks. Stock mutual funds are a preferable alternative for most people. Investing in a low-fee diversified stock mutual fund, such as Vanguard's S&P 500 index fund, will give you the superior returns of investing in stocks while significantly reducing your risk and effort.

If spending a lot of effort researching stocks to *perhaps* earn a return slightly above that of a low-fee diversified stock mutual fund does not appeal to you, you can skip this chapter. This is true because the average stock investor only earns average stock returns, the same as you could get from a diversified stock mutual fund. Therefore, it makes no sense spending effort researching stocks and learning about their intricacies unless you enjoy doing so. If that is not you, go ahead and skip this chapter 100 percent guilt-free.

I invest in individual stocks, but that is because I am a bigtime stock nerd. I enjoy spending time investigating possible stock investments and occasionally pulling the trigger on the purchase of a new stock. I am not convinced that I will earn superior returns to a diversified stock mutual fund, but I think I will. Research does not support my thought process. Historically, most investors in individual stocks have earned returns that are inferior to a low-fee S&P 500 index fund.

On the other hand, there is a ton of research that demonstrate the mistakes that individual investors commonly make. I reason that if I can avoid those mistakes, I should earn superior returns. So far, I have earned better than average returns, but nothing spectacular. I know that kind of stuff doesn't sell many books, but it is accurate, and I have done it while maintaining a safe, diversified portfolio.

I always advise investing at least $50,000 in stock mutual funds before investing in individual stocks. Starting your stock investments using mutual funds is simply the best way to achieve a diversified (safer) investment portfolio in stocks without sacrificing high returns.

After making a substantial investment in stock mutual funds, investing in individual stocks can be beneficial. You should never invest more than 10% of your portfolio in any one stock. Research indicates that a diversified portfolio requires at least 25 stocks in it to be considered safe. These stocks should be in different industries to achieve true diversification. For example, investing in 25 oil company stocks offers very little diversification.

After you have achieved a diversified stock portfolio using stock mutual funds, there are some valid reasons to invest in individual stocks. If you do not buy and sell stocks too often (you shouldn't), you can reduce taxes and fees. Once again, this takes planning and effort.

Let's look at an extremely positive example. Let's say someone bought shares in Berkshire Hathaway in 1964 and held them until 2017. I wish I had, but I was three years old at the time, and I didn't even have a stockbroker. There would have been a broker's fee in 1964 to purchase the shares. After that, there would not have been any fees or taxes. There would not have been any taxes, though. You only pay taxes when you sell your shares for a gain, or you receive a dividend (Berkshire has never paid a dividend).

The return would have been 2,404,748%. That is not a misprint. Someone who invested $1,000 in Berkshire Hathaway stock in 1964 would have stock valued at over $24 million in 2017 without paying any taxes or fees. Of course, you would have to pay capital gain taxes if you chose to sell your shares in 2017. Still, this is an example of tax and fee efficiency that is not available if you use stock mutual funds.

Another advantage of investing in stocks is that you can avoid capital gains taxes by selling a stock for a loss in the same year that you sell a stock for a gain. This is called a tax offset. Let's say you bought two stocks for $10,000 each five years ago. Now, one of those stock positions is worth $15,000, and the other is worth $5,000. You have a $5,000 gain on one stock and a $5,000 loss on the other. If you sell both of the stocks in the same year, you have zero overall profit, and thus you owe no tax.

This is called tax management. It is legal, ethical, and logical. It doesn't make any sense to pay taxes on your $5,000 gain if you are simultaneously taking a loss of $5,000. Please note that if you claim a tax loss on an investment, you are not allowed to purchase a "substantially identical" investment within 30 days before or after the sale of the original investment. This is called a wash sale and is not allowed. Also, the rules for wash sales sometimes change, so you would want to check on the latest regulations before buying and selling identical securities in a short period. The advantage of owning individual stocks is that you can manage when you take gains and losses to manage your taxes efficiently (lower your overall taxes).

It is not a good idea to invest money that you think you will need in the next few years in stocks. Stocks are too volatile to be an advisable choice for short-term (less than five years) investments. Famed investor Warren Buffett has said, "If you aren't willing to own a stock for ten years, don't even think about owning it for 10 minutes."

Let's say you want to put some money aside that you will need in three years for a new car purchase. If you invest in stocks, you won't know if you will be able to buy a new Ferrari or a used compact car. That's a lot of risk.

In the short-term, stocks are not a safe investment. In the past, stocks have performed abysmally for one, five, and ten-year periods. During the Great Depression, stocks had an average annual return of -15% annually for five years. Still, the worst yearly performance for ten years is around -2.8% annually. That's bad, but a bit less frightening.

In recent times, there have been some frightening drops in stock prices. After the internet stock bubble burst in the early 2000s, the S&P 500 stock index dropped 9.1% in 2000, then sank 11.9% in 2001, and then dropped 22.1% in 2002. At this point, any rational person would have sold all their stocks and found a safer, boring investment, wouldn't they? Many investors did just that. Those investors made a huge mistake. The S&P 500 index earned returns of 28.7% an 10.9% over the next two years. Those are outstanding returns for a two-year period.

Unfortunately, many investors sell in a panic after stocks fall and buy stocks after they have gone up a great deal. In other words, they are "selling low and buying high." That is not a good plan. It is much better to "buy low and sell high." Realistically, it is best to buy quality stocks at a reasonable price and keep the stock for years or forever.

Another more recent example of an excellent time to ignore negative stock returns and continue to invest in stocks occurred during and after the financial crisis of 2008. In 2008, the S&P 500 had a return of -37%. Yikes! Many investors yelled, "sell, sell, sell, stocks are terrible investments." They were wrong. Over the next two years, the S&P 500 index had returns of 26.5% and 15.1%.

Stocks should always be considered long-term investments. You should never panic when stock prices go down and sell because of fear. It is important to remember that you are investing in a company when you buy a stock.

Over the longer term, stocks outperform "safer" investments. Also, although high inflation is not usually beneficial to stocks, stocks do better than most investments during times of high inflation. Historically, a diversified stock portfolio has never lost money for a 20-year period. In general, stocks have a significantly higher return over the long-term than bonds, real estate, bank deposits, and other "safer" investments.

Beating the Market is Difficult

The only logical reason to invest in individual stocks instead of a low-cost stock index fund is that you think you can earn higher returns through reduced taxes and fees or superior stock picking. Saving money on taxes and fees is possible through careful planning and discipline. Beating the market through superior stock-picking is much more challenging.

One way to beat the market is to make concentrated bets on just one or a few stocks. It is also a way to incur massive losses. Investing in only a few stocks increases risk because there is a lack of diversification. Companies do go bankrupt or underperform for decades. If such a company makes up a substantial part of your portfolio, that is not cool. I heartily recommend that you do not try to beat the market by concentrating your investment in one or a few stocks.

Earning a return that is higher than a low-cost stock index fund is very difficult. In fact, most mutual funds that are actively managed by extremely intelligent, well-educated financial managers don't achieve this goal. Of course, they have expenses, and it is difficult for them to manage taxes effectively for all their clients.

Most investment managers perform worse than a low-cost stock mutual fund. So, why wouldn't you invest money with a manager that has beaten the market in the past? It turns out that this is probably not a great plan.

First, the investment manager could have just been lucky in the previous year. For example, let's say you have a competition where the 100 contestants are trying to guess heads or tails on a coin flip the most times in a row. One of the contestants wins the game by calling the correct side seven times in a row. Does this mean that the winning contestant is the best at calling coin flips and that you should bet that they will win the next contest?

Of course not. The winning contestant was just lucky. This contestant still only has a 50-50 chance of calling the next coin flip correctly. They have no particular skill. Similarly, some investment professionals get lucky one, two, three years or more in a row. They appear to be geniuses, but it is unlikely that they are earning permanently superior returns.

Historically, the mutual funds that have had the best returns from last year do worse than average over the next year. If they did better last year because of superior investment management, this should not happen. But it does.

From 1988 until 2002, the *Wall Street Journal* held a regular contest in which investment professionals picked stocks in a competition against stocks selected by throwing darts at a list of stocks from the financial pages. Undoubtedly, the investment professionals' picks would beat the random picks chosen by darts. Not so much.

The competition results were roughly equal over the years. These results mean that if you randomly chose stocks to invest in, you would be able to match the investment returns of the best, highly-paid investment professionals. To be fair, the stock competitions were for unfairly short periods, less than one year. Logically, smart investment professionals should have a harder time predicting short-term winners than predicting long-term winners. Still, the competition highlighted how hard it is to beat the market through sheer genius.

There is something called the Efficient Market Hypothesis. This theory says that stocks in the stock market are efficiently (correctly) priced based on all available information. Therefore, you are wasting your time if you try to find a stock that is a better than average investment. There is a lot of evidence that the Efficient Market Hypothesis may be correct. The fact that most active investors, investors that trade a lot, garner returns that are below that of the S&P 500 index supports the Efficient Market Hypothesis.

There is also some evidence that the Efficient Market Hypothesis is not valid. I believe that stock prices are quite efficient most of the time. If I am right, this means that it is quite challenging to beat the average return of the market, but a smart and patient investor can earn higher than average returns.

How hard is it to find an excellent investment that is highly likely to beat the market? Warren Buffett has said that if you find one great investment in a year, it's a good year. He advises that a skilled investor bypasses stocks that he is unsure of and waits for a stock in his "circle of competence" that he believes to be an excellent investment. You don't have to buy a stock, so only purchase the ones you deem the best.

Warren Buffett is perhaps the most successful investor of the last century or so. My Mom is a delightful, bright woman that knows very little about stocks. One reason that I do not fully believe in the Efficient Market Hypothesis is that to do so, I must conclude that my Mom can pick stocks as well as Warren Buffett. My apologies to the hypothesis, but I firmly believe that Buffett would be better at choosing stocks for the long-term than my Mom.

Now, this does not mean that my Mom wouldn't get lucky and beat Buffett at investing for a short time. But this is similar to me being able to beat golfing champion Jordan Spieth for one hole in golf. It could happen, but it certainly doesn't mean that I am ready for the PGA or that Spieth is not a better than average golfer.

If some investors can earn returns higher than the market averages, how can they do it? Some methods seem to work. One of the most effective ways is to avoid mistakes that cause problems for others. I believe that the best investment decision that I have made was avoiding investing in crazily priced internet-related stocks before the internet stock bubble burst. At the time, I was employed in the technology industry, and I could not fathom why some of these stocks were selling for values unrelated to revenue and earnings. Coming up with great investment ideas is terrific. Avoiding terrible investments is equally beneficial.

New investors in the stock market often get excited about tips and advice that they gather from the internet, financial publications, or paid advising services. They probably should contain their excitement. After conducting research, it is easy to think that you have gathered the information that gives you an edge over other investors. Unfortunately, it is improbable that new investors can garner knowledge that gives them an edge. Furthermore, it is quite doubtful that most experienced investors can gather knowledge through research that gives them an advantage over all other investors. Publicly available information tends to be quickly incorporated into stock prices, which makes the prices fair. The bottom line is that if you think you have inside information, you probably don't, and if you do, you can't legally use it.

Ironically, the best time to buy stocks is when the economy is sagging, and the worst time to buy is often when the economy is rocking. For example, one of the best times to buy stocks was after the financial crisis of 2008. This is easy to see in retrospect, but at the time, it was tough to buy stocks when economic and political leaders were worried about the economy collapsing. Similarly, many individuals make significant investments in the stock of the company they work for when the company's prospects look great. But, this may be the worst time to invest in the stock because many investors are aware of the company's exceptional opportunities. Ironically, this tends to increase the price of the stock to the point that it is an unwise investment.

Asset price bubbles have been occurring periodically for centuries. That's a long time and a lot of bubbles. There have already been two major asset price bubbles since the turn of the millennium (Thank goodness for spell check, I would definitely miss "millennium" in a spelling bee).

In the early 2000s, share prices of almost every stock that had anything to do with the internet soared in value. The premise behind the rise in the value of internet stocks was that the internet was going to be huge. That premise played out, and internet usage continues to soar. Unfortunately, not every company that was connected to the internet prospered.

Some companies went bankrupt: pets.com, etoys.com, and webvan.com. These companies sold pet supplies, toys, and groceries over the internet. That should have worked, but it didn't. At least, not for these companies. Other companies such as Amazon, Priceline, and eBay prospered. Still, dozens of internet bubble stocks failed, and a select few emerged as excellent investments.

I used Amazon very early on to buy books. That was their primary business at the time. I was impressed by their service, but I didn't foresee the company becoming the internet behemoth that it is today. That's one of the reasons I am writing this book instead of sipping a Mai Tai on my private tropical beach.

Later in the same decade, another financial crisis hit. During the financial crisis of 2008, home values plummeted. Millions of homeowners defaulted on their mortgages, many companies went bankrupt, and stocks lost approximately 50% of their value. Watching your stock investments go down 50% is somewhat unsettling. Gulp!

The problem with asset bubbles is that it is difficult to ascertain when a bubble exists. There are usually clues. Many skeptics predicted the internet stock and housing bubble. On the other hand, there were even more "experts" that explained why you should continue to buy internet stocks and flip houses.

After the financial crisis of 2008, many investors swore off investing in the stock market forever. That was a mistake. The broad stock market went up more than 300% over the ten years after the low point of the financial crisis. Don't make it a habit to buy high and sell low. Your goal should be to do the opposite, buy low, and sell high.

On the other hand, you should sell if an investment is unlikely to prosper in the future. If a company has a dim future, it is not a bad idea to sell and take the loss. Research shows that most people hang on to their losing investments too long. Sometimes, it is best to take a loss and move on. Also, you can shelter investment gains against taxes by realizing losses in the same year.

Disciplined Investment Strategies

"Dollar Cost Averaging" is a complicated-sounding term, and it has "averaging" right in the name, that must mean math is involved. Yes, math is required, but you don't have to do the math to benefit from dollar-cost averaging.

Millions of people use dollar-cost averaging without realizing it. Dollar-cost averaging is merely investing the same amount of money every period, with the period usually being monthly or with each paycheck. Most Americans invest in their retirement plans (401k, IRA, 403b) this way. Additionally, many choose to invest in other investments using dollar-cost averaging. That's a good thing because dollar-cost averaging has advantages that I will demonstrate now.

My example is not necessarily based on a real-world scenario, but it demonstrates how dollar-cost averaging can benefit investors in the real world. Let's say we are investing $100 a month in a stock in each of the next 12 months. Furthermore, let's assume the price of the stock when we purchase it in each of the next twelve months is shown in this table:

Month Purchased	Price	Shares Purchased
Jan	$25	4.00
Feb	$20	5.00
Mar	$15	6.67
Apr	$20	5.00
May	$25	4.00
Jun	$35	2.86
Jul	$35	2.86
Aug	$30	3.33
Sep	$25	4.00
Oct	$20	5.00
Nov	$25	4.00
Dec	$30	3.33
Total Shares Purchased		**50.05**

Notice that in months when the price of the stock is down, more shares are purchased. Similarly, when the price of the stock is up, fewer shares are purchased. Thus, we are buying more shares when the price is low and fewer shares when the price is high. That's a good thing because we are accomplishing the first part of the investors' creed of "buy low and sell high." This is a significant advantage of dollar-cost averaging.

In our example, we purchased a little over 50 shares. If we had used the entire $1,200 that we invested during the year in January, we would have bought only 48 shares at $25. Also, if we had chosen to invest the entire $1,200 in August, we would have only been able to purchase 40 shares at $30. Clearly, owning 50 shares is better than 48 or 40.

On the other hand, if we had timed things better and invested our entire $1,200 in February, we would have been able to purchase 60 shares at $20. Whoops, owning 60 shares is better than the 50 we would have bought through dollar-cost averaging. Therefore, if we can time the market so that we purchase shares when the price of the shares is at or near their low point, we can do better than dollar-cost averaging.

Unfortunately, it is extremely difficult to determine when a stock is at its low point. Therefore, dollar cost averaging lowers our risk while ensuring that we buy more shares when the price of the stock is low than we do when the price of the stock is high. We lower our risk while ensuring that we are purchasing most of our shares when the price lower than average. This is why most investment advisors recommend that investors invest their money regularly. Dollar-cost averaging is a good, lower-risk strategy for most investors.

It should be noted that dollar-cost averaging is more effective in purchasing mutual funds that generally move with the market and rarely go to zero than in buying individual stocks. This is because a single stock's price can go to zero and stay there if the company goes bankrupt. In this scenario, dollar-cost averaging would not save you from losing your entire investment.

Still, dollar-cost averaging into reliable mutual funds as most people do in their retirement investments is a robust and recommended strategy for almost everyone.

When investing in stocks, one of the best ways to do better than the average investors is to avoid common mistakes that many investors make. Failing to diversify investments adequately is a widespread mistake. Diversification requires investing in a wide array of assets. A typical diversified portfolio would include stocks, real estate, and bonds. It is important to remember that if you own a home or other land for your personal use, that is also an investment.

When investing in stocks or stock mutual funds, diversification is particularly important. It is not advisable to invest in only a few stocks or a few industries. If investing in individual stocks, diversify your investments across several industries. Don't invest in mutual funds concentrated in an industry unless you have other mutual funds that will provide diversification.

The easiest way to diversify stock investments is to invest the majority of your stock-related investments into a widely diversified stock mutual fund such as an S&P 500 index fund. If you choose to only invest in individual stocks, sufficient diversification can be obtained by investing in 30 – 50 stocks in several different industries.

A simple way to think of diversification is that you are not putting all your eggs in one basket. That way, if you drop one of the baskets, all is not lost. Concentrating your investment in only one or two stocks can indeed reap incredible returns if one of these stocks has tremendous gains. On the other hand, this lack of diversification can easily lead to terrible losses, including losing everything. It is irrational to fail to diversify your investments properly.

Checking on your investments would seem like a wise thing to do, but that is not always true. It is smart to monitor your finances regularly. But it is not a great idea to monitor long-term investments on a daily or weekly basis. Checking investments too frequently can result in anxiety and poor decisions.

For example, let's look at a working person in their fifties that has $1,000,000 invested in stocks in their retirement portfolio. This person goes to work on a typical weekday and earns $400 (before taxes). Then, they come home, check their portfolio, and find their stock investments went down 1% that day, a common daily outcome. They then do some quick math and realize that their retirement investment was down $10,000 in one day. Now, work seems unimportant. Anxiety and depression set in. Worse, the person may decide they don't want to risk their portfolio having a negative return. Therefore, they move their retirement savings into a low-risk and extremely low-return investment.

Short-term investments, those in which the money will be needed in less than five or ten years, should be low risk. The value of long-term investments should fluctuate a significant amount because that is the nature of high return investments like the stock market. It is not exceptionally unusual for the stock market to go down 20%, 30%, or even more over a two- or three-year period. Still, it is almost always a bad idea to bail out of these investments after they have gone down. Remember, the goal is to buy low and sell high. If you sell your investments after they have gone down a great deal, you are selling low. In other words, you are often selling when it is a great time to buy.

Monitor your long-term investments, such as retirement plans monthly, quarterly, or yearly. Don't fret overly about fluctuations in value because they will happen. Above all, don't panic and sell when your investments are at a low point.

Beta is a measure of how much a stock's price fluctuates. A higher beta means the stock price varies more. Many college instructors teach students that stocks with a higher beta earn higher returns. Many college texts state that this is true. One problem, research indicates this is not true. In reality, higher beta stocks tend to have slightly lower returns than lower beta stocks. Theoretically, this should not occur. My money is on reality. My advice is to ignore a stock's beta as a factor in your investment decisions.

Technical analysts are often called chartists. Chartists use charts of a stock's past price movements and volume of shares sold to predict what the stock will do in the future. Technical analysts are often featured in investment articles, websites, and television shows. Many technical analysts make fortunes selling their predictions. Some of them become minor celebrities.

Unfortunately, there is very little evidence that technical analysts can beat the market averages. There is a lot of research indicating that technical analysts do not beat the market. Still, some of these analysts are always doing well during any given time. During these periods, the technical analysts that are doing well will end up being featured prominently in the media and advertisements. That doesn't mean you should follow their advice. I don't know any technical analysts that have excelled for extended periods. My advice is to treat technical analysis as entertainment, not practical investment advice.

Some stock "experts" advise using stop-loss orders. Stop-loss orders mandate selling a stock if its price falls to a certain point. For example, an investor that owns stock with a current price of $100 might put in a stop-loss order at $90. In this case, if the stock price drops to $90, the stock would automatically be sold.

The logic behind the stop-loss order in this example is that it limits the loss on the investment to $10 (10%). It seems like a good idea to limit damages in this manner. The problem is that the stop-loss locks in a loss. The stop-loss order initiates a sell when the price of the stock reaches a certain low point. It causes the investor to sell low.

If the stock continues to sink, the stop-loss is a good thing. On the other hand, if the stock recovers and moves up, as stocks often do. All we accomplish with the stop-loss order is selling our stock at a low point. Selling low is not our goal. Therefore, I do not advise using stop-loss orders in the vast majority of circumstances.

There is strong evidence that most investors hold onto their losing stock investments too long and sell their winning stock investments too soon. Once I learned of this typical irrational investing behavior, I reviewed my finances and realized that I was guilty of this mistake.

The rationale behind decisions of this type sounds rational. The justification for selling winners too soon is, "I have made a lot of money on this investment, now I can sell it and lock in my gain." Yes, you indeed lock in a gain, but that does not mean that you aren't giving up substantial future profits. If you invested early in Microsoft, Amazon, or Apple and sold after you earned a 30%, 50%, or 100% return, that was a good investment. But it could have been so much better.

The rationale behind holding on to losers too long is "if I hold on until the investment earns a positive return, I haven't lost money." The problem with this rationale is that the investment may not return to a profitable position *ever*. The investment may languish for years or decades with a negative return, or the value of the investment may even go to zero. Personally, two smallish stock investments that I have had went to zero as the companies declared bankruptcy. After those negative 100% returns on investment, I vowed to do all I could to avoid riding a company's stock down to zero. Yes, they were small investments, but it still was painful to lose the entire investment.

Theoretically, we should not pay any attention to our past returns on an investment. This theory is logical because what we paid for an investment in the past is irrelevant. Past investment costs that are not going to change no matter what we do are called sunk costs and should be ignored. The only exception is if we are considering selling a stock for tax management purposes. If we are selling a stock for a profit, we may want to sell another stock for a loss to offset this gain for tax purposes (and vice versa).

Unfortunately, ignoring sunk costs is difficult psychologically. Similarly, resisting the urge to sell a winner to lock in a win is also challenging. Still, logic should rule. The relevant question is, "would this be an acceptable investment to me if I was purchasing a new investment today?" If the answer is no, the investment should be sold. If the answer is yes, the investment should be held. Of course, tax implications should be considered in these decisions.

Let's summarize. Tax implications should be considered but should not generally drive investment decisions. Sell a stock only when it is very far removed from the type of stock you'd buy if you were buying today. Resist the urge to hold on to losers too long and to sell winners too early.

There are diversification benefits to investing in countries other than the USA. It is often true that investments in other countries do well when investments in the USA do poorly and vice versa. This effect tends to smooth out returns, essentially lowering risk without significantly reducing returns.

Most financial advisors, including me, recommend investing some of your funds into international investments. The primary benefit of international investing is the diversification factor. There are disadvantages, though. Foreign investments often have higher costs. Also, taxes on international investments can be somewhat complicated and can often lower the after-tax return on the investment. Also, the benefit of international diversification has often disappeared during past periods of financial distress at precisely the time when they are most needed.

Notably, investing in American corporations that earn a large portion of their sales and profits overseas provides a significant amount of international diversification. Companies such as McDonalds, Coca Cola, and IBM fall into this category.

Despite the problems of investing internationally, the benefits are considerable. I keep a portion of my long-term investments invested overseas. I suggest that you do the same.

Many companies pay dividends to their stockholders. Many do not. Dividends are an important reason to own stocks. After all, there are only two ways to make money from owning stocks: receiving dividends or selling the stock for more than you bought it.

There are many reasons why a company may choose to pay a dividend or not. Companies that are in dire financial straits rarely pay a dividend. On the other hand, successful companies with rapid growth in sales and earnings don't usually pay a dividend. Instead, they tend to reinvest all their profits into further growth of the company. For example (as of 2019), fantastically successful companies such as Amazon, Facebook, and Alphabet (Google) have never paid a dividend.

Also, some companies choose not to pay a dividend in the name of tax efficiency. Berkshire Hathaway is one of the most successful and profitable companies of the last 60 years. Yet, Berkshire has never paid a dividend. The company doesn't want to force a dividend on investors, thus forcing the investors to pay income tax on the dividend. Instead, investors can choose to sell their stock when they want or need the money and pay a tax on their capital gains.

This way, investors that don't need income can let the value of their investment in the stock grow tax-deferred for decades.

More mature companies with steady profits tend to pay dividends. Most, but not all, companies that pay dividends tend to be safer investment options. There are two critical measures of dividends. The first is the dividend yield, and the second is the payout ratio. The dividend yield of individuals stocks is widely available on the internet and other sources. Dividend yield is the annual dividend of a share of stock divided by the price per share of the stock. It is expressed in a percentage and can be interpreted as the yearly percentage cash return on an investment in the stock.

For example, if a company had a stock price of $100 and paid four quarterly dividends of 75 cents over the past year ($3 for the whole year), the dividend yield would be 3.00%. For investors dependent on income from their investments, the dividend yield is an important ratio.

Many companies regularly raise their dividends. Companies that have raised their dividends every year for a decade or more are often called "dividend aristocrats." Dividend aristocrats have historically been steady, profitable investments. There are many mutual funds and exchange-traded funds (ETFs) that only invest in dividend aristocrats. These are a safe choice for investors that want a steady income that will rise faster than the inflation rate.

The second measure of dividends is the payout ratio. The payout ratio is the annual dividends paid divided by the yearly earnings. The payout ratio is not as widely reported as dividend yield, but it is available. The payout ratio is a determinant of the likelihood that a company will be able to continue to pay and increase the dividend.

For example, if a company paid dividends per share of $4.00 over the past year and had earnings per share (EPS) of $8.00, the payout ratio would be 50%. Fifty percent of the profits would be paid out in dividends to the shareholders. The other 50% of the earnings would be reinvested in the company for the benefit of the shareholders.

A lower payout ratio indicates that a firm has the financial strength to be able to continue paying dividends or even raise the dividend. As a payout ratio approaches or even exceeds 100%, this indicates that the firm is more likely not to be able to increase the dividend or be forced to cut or discontinue the dividend. Most firms cut their dividend as a last resort. Dividend cuts are viewed unfavorably by most investors and usually result in the stock price going down dramatically.

Investors that are interested in investing in dividend stocks should pay attention to these two dividend measures. A higher dividend yield indicates a higher cash income return on the investment. A lower payout ratio indicates that the company is more likely to continue paying a dividend or even raise the dividend.

In general, the management of companies that pay dividends want to keep paying the dividends and raise them consistently. Investors who choose to invest in dividend-paying companies often view dividend cuts as a good reason to sell the stock. If the stock price goes down as a result of dividend cuts (which usually happens), management suffers from increased stress, decreased compensation, and potential job loss. Therefore, management often strives to make sure they can continue to pay the dividend. Theoretically, the managers in dividend-paying companies work harder to ensure they can keep paying the dividend and keep their jobs. There is evidence to support this theory.

Another advantage of owning dividend stocks is that the dividends can be soothing to investors during stock market downturns. When the market turns down ten, twenty, or thirty percent or more, it is easier to hang on to your stock investments and not sell in a panic when your dividend payments continue to keep coming. Dividend payments do tend to continue even during bad economic times because most firms' management works hard to make sure they can keep paying the dividend.

For example, most firms either increased or maintained their dividend during the financial crisis of 2008. Few investors remained unnerved when they saw their stock investments fall dramatically during the crisis. It was easier to not sell in a panic if your stock dividend income did not plummet.

If you have stock investments in both a tax-deferred retirement account (401k, 403b, IRA, etc.) and taxable account, the choice of where you own dividend and non-dividend stocks is an important financial decision. If you need income, owning dividend stocks in your taxable account makes sense. If you do not need current income, it makes more sense to hold dividend stocks in your tax-deferred account. These tactics will minimize your taxes.

Different Types of Stock: Value, Growth, Small-Cap, and Large-Cap

Historically, some types of stocks have earned a higher return than other stocks over the long-term (sometimes only over the very long-term). If historical patterns persist in the future, investors that take advantage of these stock return differentials can earn a substantially higher return on their long-term investments.

Let me put the previous paragraph more succinctly. If you buy the right kind of stocks, you will be much wealthier in retirement. That's what we in the investment biz call incentive.

Over the past 100 plus years, value stocks have had higher returns than growth stocks. Value stocks generally have a lower stock price to earnings per share (P/E) ratios and lower stock price to accounting book value per share (P/B) ratios. Value stocks generally tend to have lower growth rates in sales and earnings. These types of stock are designated as "value" stocks because the investor is thought to be getting a good value by purchasing the stock's sales and earnings at a low or "value" price.

Conversely, growth stocks generally have higher price-earnings (P/E) ratios and higher price to book (P/B) ratios. Also, growth stocks tend to have higher growth rates in sales and earnings, hence the "growth stock" moniker. Over the past 100-plus years, value stocks have had higher returns than growth stocks. Depending on the long-term period measured, value stocks have tended to earn about 1% per year more than growth stocks.

Much like the differentiation between value and growth stocks, the stocks of smaller companies have earned higher average returns than the stocks of larger companies over the last 100-plus years. Smaller companies have a smaller market capitalization. Market capitalization (market cap) is the value of all of the company's stock shares (stock price times the number of shares). In general, stocks are broken down into three categories based on the size of the company: small-cap, mid-cap, and large-cap.

Over the past 100-plus years, small-cap stocks have had higher returns than large-cap stocks. In general, small-cap stocks have earned around 2% more per year than large-cap stocks over the long-term. Importantly, small-cap stock prices are usually significantly more volatile than the stock price of large-cap stocks. This means that small-cap stock prices fall much more during market downtrends and rise much more during good times. This volatility can be unnerving to the average investor.

The slight average yearly return advantage garnered from investing in value and small-cap stocks versus investing in growth, and large-cap stocks may not seem like a big deal. After all, a one or two percent difference return in a given year is not a big deal. But, over a forty- or fifty-year period, a difference in an annual return of 1% or 2% is dramatic, perhaps a difference of hundreds of thousands of dollars.

The long-term trends in the value vs. growth stock and small-cap vs. large-cap stock returns seem persistent, but the patterns can often be reversed for several years. In other words, it is not uncommon for growth stocks to provide better returns than value stocks for 10-year periods or more. Similarly, large-cap stocks can outperform small-cap stocks for an extended number of years.

The financial industry is well aware of the long-term trends related to value versus growth and market capitalization. Therefore, much attention is paid to these issues. Mutual funds based on these factors are common. One can purchase mutual funds that invest in small-cap, mid-cap, large-cap, value, growth, small-cap value, small-cap growth, large-cap value, and large-cap growth stocks. Of course, extended market index funds that invest in all of these types of stocks are available. Investing in an extended market index fund of this type is hard to argue with because it will probably provide a relatively high return over the long-term with little long-term risk.

The world and economic frameworks are ever-changing. Therefore, the relative returns of value and growth stocks and small-cap and large-cap stocks may be different over the next hundred years. I am banking on the future resembling the past. Therefore, I have invested a significant portion of my retirement savings in small-cap value funds. I also have a considerable part of my long-term investments in extended market index funds. I would advise you to do the same.

Over the last hundred plus years, value stocks have earned a significantly higher return than growth stocks. In general, value stocks have slower, or no growth in earnings and sales and growth stocks have higher *growth* (thus the name) in earnings and sales. Value stocks get their name from the thought that they are a good *value* because these stocks can be bought for a lower multiple of their earnings and sales. In other words, you pay less for a dollar of earnings if you purchase a value stock.

Let's look at a realistic example. Let's imagine that there are two stocks, each with a dollar per-share earnings over the last year. One of these stocks (stock G) has a share price of $20, and the other (stock V) has a share price of $10. The price-to-earnings (P/E) ratio is perhaps the most commonly used valuation ratio for stocks.

In this case, if we took stock G's share price of $20 and divided it by its earnings per share of $1, we find that stock G has a P/E ratio of 20. Similarly, stock V has a P/E ratio of 10. This means that if we buy stock G, we are paying $20 for each dollar of earnings. On the other hand, if we buy stock V, we are only paying $10 for each dollar of earnings. If we purchase stock V, we are spending half as much per dollar of earnings. Stock V is a better value because we can buy a dollar of earnings at a lower price.

But the story doesn't end there. Now, the question is why anyone would buy stock G if a dollar of G's earning cost twice as much as a dollar of V's earnings. There is only one logical explanation. Investors expect stock G's future earnings to grow at a faster rate than stock V's future earnings. This is the crux of the difference between value and growth stocks. Purchasing a value stock gets us more profits today, while a growth stock gets us the expectation of more profits in the future.

So why have value stocks earned a higher return than growth stocks over the *very* long-term? This is the subject of much debate. I will give you the story I believe to be true. Value stocks have low future expectations cooked into their stock price. Therefore, if they exceed expectations, the stock price goes up.

On the other hand, growth stocks have optimistic future expectations. Therefore, if growth companies fall short of their predicted bright future, the stock price goes down. Also, growth companies are generally exciting investments that make great cocktail party conversation, value stocks not so much. Would you rather be involved in a conversation about an impressive high-tech growth stock or a value stock of a company that sold gravel? The excitement about growth stocks tends to increase its current stock price, which makes it more difficult for the stock price to grow even more in the future.

Please note that it is not uncommon for growth stocks to earn higher returns than value stocks for ten- or twenty-year periods. Still, over the long-term value stocks have done better.

There are many different ways to define value stocks. I already mentioned the P/E ratio. It is important to note that not all P/E ratios are equal. Sometimes the ratio is calculated using past reported earnings. Trailing P/E ratios use past earnings. Sometimes the P/E ratio is computed using forecasted earnings. This is called a forward P/E ratio. When comparing two companies, it is essential to compare using the same type of P/E ratio.

Value stocks are also often classified based on price-to-sales (P/S) ratios, price-to-book (P/B) ratios, and dividend yield. Determining which stocks are actual values and which ones are so-called "value traps" is difficult and requires some homework. Value traps are stocks that are priced low for a reason, and their stock price does not go up because the companies have real problems.

P/E ratios for the market and individual stocks vary a great deal over time. It is generally better to buy when these are low (when stocks are on sale). Some great companies can be terrible investments if you pay too high a price for the stock. On the other hand, some high P/E growth stocks can be great investments. For example, a Lamborghini is a fantastic car, but if you paid $50 million for a new one, that would not be a great purchase. If instead, you paid $20,000 for one, that would be sweet. For stocks and cars, it is not only the quality of the product, but the price also matters a great deal.

Even if you think you are great at picking out undervalued companies, diversify across stocks and industries because you could be wrong. You will almost certainly get it wrong sometimes. I have invested in 2 companies that went bankrupt. I have always had widely diversified investments, so losing everything in an individual investment did not have a significant impact on my overall returns. Still, it was not fun, and I hope it never happens again.

Blue-chip, seemingly safe companies sometimes go bankrupt. Here's just a few that were thought to be perfectly safe a few years before bankruptcy: Enron, WorldCom, Texaco, General Motors, and Lehman Brothers.

Even the great investor Warren Buffett has had some real losers. He has way more winners, and his investments are widely diversified. I am not trying to deter you from investing in stocks. My point is that everyone makes mistakes, but proper diversification will prevent disaster.

Chapter 10 – The Essentials: If You Only Read One Chapter, Read This One

What is This Chapter About?

I have learned that many people do not want to read a whole book on personal finance. It seems overwhelming and confusing. Therefore, I have added this summary chapter on the essentials of personal finance. Reading a chapter on personal finance is much easier than reading a book. If you have read the earlier chapters, good job! This chapter should be a useful review for you.

If you decided not to read the earlier chapters and skip to this chapter, that is okay. The most critical points of the book are here. If you only read this chapter, you will know enough to move towards financial success. After reading this chapter, you may decide to go back and read the rest of the book. That is my hope, and I advise that you do so.

After this chapter, I have included an appendix which consists of a one-page list of steps to financial success suitable for bulletin boards and refrigerator magnets. I hope everyone that reads this book will post this list as a reminder of their goals. If you follow the steps regularly (most of us slip up occasionally), you will be much more likely to achieve your financial goals.

You Control Your Financial Destiny

You may not be in an acceptable financial situation. It is meaningful for you to know that you control your financial future. Being in control is good, but it is not always easy. There are things that you need to do to improve your financial future and success. First, educate yourself on personal finance essentials. Reading this book will accomplish that.

You also need to continue learning about personal finance for the rest of your life. You don't need to be an expert, but you should continue to be aware of significant changes in taxes and other financial matters. Also, you need to make a financial plan and use it.

You must work to save up 3 to 6 months' worth of living expenses in emergency savings. This may be a challenging goal, but it is a crucial one. A watershed moment in my financial independence journey was the realization that I had saved enough money to deal with the typical emergencies of everyday life, such as a car breaking down. This realization felt very good. Proper emergency savings turn a catastrophe into an annoyance. That leads to a significant life improvement.

This first step of saving for emergencies can seem impossible if you have seemingly insurmountable debts. Still, if you are in this situation, there are numerous sources of help that will not charge you a fee. Seek advice from these organizations.

The best part of controlling your financial future is that gaining control of your finances gives you the freedom to improve your life. Freedom is great, but it comes with responsibilities. The first responsibility is to start building up your savings and remember that: ***"If you don't save money, you will always be poor!"***

Lifestyle Decisions are Also Important Financial Decisions

Education is a significant investment of money, time, and effort. If your education allows you to pursue a rewarding career that you enjoy, it will be the best investment you ever make. Importantly, if you decide to attend college, the most crucial goal is to graduate.

Choosing a career is a challenging and essential decision. The decision should weigh the importance of income, benefits, work conditions, and job enjoyment. You should evaluate career options at least once a year. Changing careers is not easy, but sometimes it is the best path.

The choice of a spouse or life-partner is a critical one that has enormous financial implications. Choose wisely, and do not ignore the economic consequences. If you are single, never date someone with more problems than you (this is possibly the best advice I have ever received).

Don't have children until you can afford to take care of them. Children are expensive, but an investment of time and money in them can result in unexplainably beautiful rewards. If you have kids, teach your kids about making sound financial decisions.

Divorce is expensive and painful. If you have to get divorced, put your kids' needs first. They are innocent. In the event of a divorce, protect your financial interests. Things can get ugly quickly.

Avoid vampire friends and relatives, those that are regularly taking from you and not giving back. This does not mean that you should not help friends and relatives that have fallen on hard times. It does mean that you should not allow capable friends and relatives to take from you while giving you little in return continually. If there are friends that are dragging you down, you should reevaluate your relationship with them.

Don't loan money to friends or relatives. If you want to help a loved one in need, give them a gift. Loans often harm relationships, but gifts rarely do.

It is a good idea to become friends with successful people that you like and admire. Networking is not a bad word; it is okay when friends help their friends that they trust.

If a relationship or an action doesn't make you money or make you happy in the long run, consider not continuing the relationship or committing the action. In other words, don't do things that don't benefit you.

Budget, Goals, and Debt

Money can't buy happiness, but it does make it more likely.

Creating and *using* a budget is *essential* to financial success. Essential means "you gotta do it." If you enjoy simple pleasures and limited possessions, it is much easier to lead an enjoyable life and keep to a budget.

Traditional budgets work, and there is a lot of information available to help you to implement them. If you prefer to use a reverse budget, reverse budgets can be a beneficial and easy budgeting technique. The important thing is that you choose to use either a traditional budget or a reverse budget. More importantly, you need to *use* the budget every month.

Open a checking account and a savings account and balance your checking account monthly. You can quickly learn how to balance your checking account on the web. You do not ever want to bounce a check because it can severely damage your credit and cost you a great deal of money in fees.

Steady financial progress is a rewarding experience that often facilitates happiness. The first step to making steady progress is to make short-term and long-term financial goals and evaluate your progress regularly. Also, calculate your net worth annually and assess your progress towards your goals.

Make short-term financial goals using the SMART technique. The goals should be: (Specific, Measurable, Achievable, Realistic, and Time-based). Evaluate your goals regularly and make changes and new goals based on your results.

When formulating your budget and goals, you should ignore sunk costs. This means that money and time that you have already spent on past relationships, investments, education, and other expenses are gone. You can't recover that money or time. Therefore, these sunk costs should not have an impact on your decisions going forward. Ignoring sunk costs is not easy emotionally, but it is the logical thing to do.

Here is the most important rule about using credit cards: ***Pay your credit card balances in full every month***. If you do this, you will not have to pay any interest on your credit card purchases. The best way to build credit is to pay off all your bills on time every time. Misuse of credit cards is one of the most common causes of bankruptcy. Don't let it happen to you.

Once you can qualify for major credit cards (Visa, MasterCard, American Express, or Discovery), you should have three major credit cards. At least one of these cards should be either Visa or MasterCard because numerous businesses do not accept American Express or Discovery. If you can get a cash rewards credit card, do it.

Every year, you can request one free credit report from each of the three major credit agencies (Equifax, TransUnion, and Experian). Banks and credit card companies often offer free credit reports to their customers. You should check on your credit once a year.

Reduce Expenses

Saving money requires earning more than you spend. So, if you are not saving money, you either need to spend less money or make more money. You can do it if you search for ways to cut expenses and make more money.

Small changes in behavior can make significant differences over the long-term. For example, if you either save or make (after tax) $2.75 more a day, that works out to a $1,000 difference over a year. This is money you can save or invest. Therefore, you should regularly be looking for opportunities to improve your every day or every-month financial decisions.

You should have a checking account and some type of savings account. You should shop for financial services that have the lowest fees. Also, if you need to borrow money, shop for the lowest interest rates. Join a credit union. Be wary of loans or investments that sound too good to be true.

Shop around for any recurring expense such as home insurance, car insurance, apartments, internet service, phone service, and gym memberships. A difference of $75 a month in rent doesn't sound that big, but a difference of $900 a year does even though they are the same thing.

I want you to save your money, but there are some crucial areas where you should not skimp. One of these areas is safety and security.

Quitting or cutting back on vices is a fabulous way to save money. It is rare to save money while improving your life. Omitting vices is one such way. If you are not going to quit your vice, cut back and save as much as possible while continuing your wicked ways ☺.

Pets can bring great joy, but they also can bring great expense. Do not take on the responsibility of owning a pet without considerable forethought.

Vacations, especially family vacations, are essential. Vacations are times to recharge the batteries, relax, enjoy, and build memories. Vacations should not be something that causes one to lose their home, go into crushing debt, lose educational opportunities, risk a comfortable retirement, or endure bankruptcy. So, plan reasonable vacations that you can afford. Don't purchase a vacation timeshare. There are just too many risks involved.

A hobby that you enjoy that costs nothing is a great hobby.

Taking care of your health through exercise, healthy eating, and other healthy habits can not only make you feel better but also save you money.

Extended warranties are almost always a bad idea.

You should think of your housing choice as both a lifestyle and a financial decision. Purchasing a home is a practical way to build wealth and stability. You should not buy a home unless you are reasonably sure that you want to live in that home for at least five years.

If you decide to buy a home, I highly recommend that you do _not_ buy the most expensive house you can afford. Buy the least expensive home that will best meet your needs and wants. I also advise buying one of the lower-cost homes in fully-developed neighborhoods in excellent school districts. This advice holds even if you do not have kids because the marvelous school district will make it easier to resell your home at a higher price. Also, if you have or plan to have kids, a house with access to good public schools can save you hundreds of thousands of dollars of private school tuition.

Your mortgage selection is a meaningful financial decision that can go a long way towards making a satisfactory housing purchase. The importance of the work commute should not be underestimated in the home purchasing decision. When it comes time to sell your home, do your homework and make your home as attractive a value as possible. Selling a home is stressful, and that stress can be relieved if you sell relatively quickly at a higher price.

A good roommate can be a beautiful thing. Sharing expenses with a roommate can _significantly_ improve your finances. Ideally, your roommate can be a friend that will enhance your life in other ways. I would advise against moving in with your significant other if saving money is in your top three reasons for moving in together. Cohabitating is a decision that should not rely significantly on a financial rationale.

Transportation, including automobiles, is a reoccurring expense. The reoccurrence factor increases the importance of keeping transportation expenses under control. If you buy a car, don't buy a new one unless you are rich. The easiest way to improve safety is to drive safely and avoid unnecessary trips in the car. Lowering your mileage will also save you money. Automobile insurance is a considerable reoccurring expense, so shop around for it.

You should start saving for your children's education at a very early age. A 529 plan is the best way to save for a child's college. Do not use retirement savings to pay for a child's education.

College decisions are complicated and should be thoroughly researched. The financial impact on parents and children is enormous. The primary factor in school choice is to attend one that that you are highly likely to complete your education. The second most crucial college decision is the choice of a major. The goal of going to college should be to graduate with a major that will lead to a satisfying career with as little debt as possible.

Investment Fundamentals

Your first savings goal should be to have 3 to 6 months' worth of living expenses in emergency savings. Emergency savings should be deposited in a safe investment, such as an FDIC-insured account.

Longer-term investments, money not needed for five years or more, should be invested in stocks and bonds. It is relevant to know what stocks and bonds are. If you buy a bond, you are lending money to a company or a government. If you buy a share of common stock, you become a part-owner of a company.

Most people should not invest in individual stocks and bonds. It is better to invest in stock and bond mutual funds. If you have a retirement plan at your employer such as a 401(k), 403(b), or similar program, you will probably have the option to invest in different mutual funds. Mutual funds pool funds from many investors to invest in a diversified portfolio of stocks or bonds or both. Some mutual funds invest in other assets. The best type of mutual fund for almost all investors is a low-cost, no-load index fund.

This book is not designed to help budding entrepreneurs. If you want to start your own business, I encourage you to do so. Still, please do your homework before you get started to increase your chances of success.

Avoid scams and dubious investment plans. You should never make an investment based on a cold call from someone you don't have a pre-existing business relationship. Making an upfront investment in a multi-level marketing plan that requires you to sell products to your friends and recruit others is usually a terrible idea.

Many financial scammers have relationships or ties that they exploit to gain their victims' trust. For example, they use religious or ethnic relations. Most of us want to trust members of our church or people that hail from our home country. The scammers know this and take advantage of it. The bottom line is that if an investment sounds too good to be true, it probably is not true. Don't let greed drive you towards becoming a victim, especially if the person selling you the investment is not attached to a well-known and reputable financial company.

Essential Financial Tasks

TCB! That means that you should be "Taking Care of Business. In personal finance, TCB means ensuring that your insurance, will, and taxes are in order.

If you have a spouse, children, or anyone else that depends on you financially, you need to buy life insurance. A commonly used rule of thumb for life insurance is to purchase insurance coverage equivalent to six to ten times your annual salary. You can adjust this for other factors, but I advise erring on the side of too much coverage.

Term life insurance is the least expensive type of life insurance. As long as you are not very wealthy, term life insurance is the only type of life insurance you should purchase. As with any other significant expense, shop around for life insurance. Please don't leave your financially dependent loved ones unprotected in case something happens to you.

Another thing you need to do to protect your loved ones is creating a will. If you do not have a will, the state will decide how your estate is distributed and who will take care of your children. Additionally, changing account owners, ownership of cars, deed owners, and other critical legal changes are much more difficult for your spouse and children if you don't have a proper will. An invalid will is no better than no will at all. Please make a proper will so that your loved ones are not burdened with *attempting* to straighten out your affairs as they are grieving.

Health, disability, automobile, homeowner's, and renter's insurance are also types of protection that most people need. These insurance plans can provide financial stability when disaster strikes. The need for these insurance plans varies significantly from person to person. The price can also vary considerably based on individual factors, shopping around, and deductibles. To take care of business, you must evaluate your need for these insurances and act accordingly.

Insurance is a reoccurring expense. Therefore, the importance of managing this expense increases. Make sure you have adequate coverage but pay as little as you can for the coverage you need.

You should pay your taxes, and you should pay them on time. To do otherwise invites negative financial consequences and other potential limitations on your freedoms. In other words, you might get fined or go to jail. We don't want that.

Paying income taxes is not all bad; it means you're making money. There are some positive ways to lower your taxes legally and ethically. Tax preferred investments that encourage saving for retirement or college, such as IRAs, 401(k)s, 403(b)s, and 529s are almost always excellent investment opportunities with significant long-term tax advantages.

There are only two possibilities when you do not file your taxes. Either you are passing up a tax return (bad), or you owe money that you are not paying (worse). The penalties for not filing a tax return include fines, high-interest payments, a criminal record, and jail time. File your taxes every year.

The tax code is ever-changing. Most changes in the tax code don't dramatically change the financial plan of the average person. Even so, financial plans and options must be re-evaluated regularly, especially when significant tax changes take effect.

Giving your time or money to charity is something you should do. When it comes to charity, "don't give until it hurts, give until it feels good." You should pick a charity and cause you are familiar with, so you know your money will be spent to actually help people and not just end up in some fundraiser's pocket. It has been my experience that giving time and money to charity benefits me as much or more than it does the ones I am helping. As your wealth increases, you should have the resources to give more to charity.

Financial advisors are first and foremost sales professionals. If they are paid on commission, they are incentivized to generate more commissions. This misguided incentive is the main reason that most other financial experts and I recommend that you use a fee-only financial advisor.

If you are not yet wealthy, it may *not* be a good idea to use a fee-only financial advisor because the fixed fee is usually over $500. If they are satisfactory advisors and you have substantial investments, this is money well spent. If you have less than $100,000 to invest, a financial advisor that is paid a portion of the money you invest or earn on your investment can be a suitable choice. As long as a financial advisor is open about how they are compensated, you should be able to understand how you are benefiting from their advice and how they are benefitting as well.

You should not blindly trust anyone providing you financial advice. You must understand your finances, any information you receive, and the impact of the financial decisions you are making. It is the job of the financial advisor to help you to understand all of this.

If you do not understand an investment, don't make it. You should be able to explain to a 12-year-old why you are making a financial decision. Financial laws, economic factors, and personal financial situations change continually, so there is no such thing as knowing everything you will ever need to know about finance. Still, having a trusted financial planner is a great idea for almost everyone at some point.

Plan for Retirement, Start Early

The primary goal of saving for retirement is to save enough to have your savings reach a level of "critical mass," in which your retirement savings are earning more each year than you are withdrawing to meet your financial needs. If you reach critical mass, you will never run out of money. This goal is lofty, but it should be your goal.

Don't rely on life expectancy statistics to determine how much money you will need. If your life expectancy at retirement is 12 years and you save accordingly, living 30 years could become a problem. Running out of money when you are retired is a severe problem. Having more money than you need when you are retired is a beautiful problem.

Some version of Social Security will almost certainly be around when you retire, even if you are very young. You should not rely on receiving substantial income from Social Security when you retire. Still, you can probably count on getting enough money from your government benefits to live a lifestyle at or just above the poverty level.

Deciding when to begin collecting Social Security benefits is a complicated decision that depends on many factors such as marital status, age, spouse's age, health, spouse's health, life expectancy, ability to work, and income needs. Do your homework, and do not take this decision lightly.

You should start saving for your retirement when you are young. The younger, the better. Simply put, a 401(k), 403(b), 457, Thrift Savings Plan (TSP) or similar retirement plan with employer matching contributions is an unbelievably good investment and the surest way to long-term wealth building. If you do not have access to one of these plans, you should contribute money to another retirement plan, such as an IRA regularly.

When you participate in an employer-matching plan, you are essentially getting free money because your employer contributes money to your retirement account that you would otherwise not receive. If you have the option to participate in one of these employer-matching retirement plans, you should do so. I can rarely give unconditional advice like this, but you do not want to forgo free money. ***Make sure you are contributing as much money as your employer will match.*** Don't turn down "free money."

Here is a plan for success if you have access to a 401(k) or similar program. At the start of your career, find a way to invest enough in your company's 401(k) to garner all of the employer matching contributions available to you. Secondly, every time you get a raise (which tends to happen more often early in your career), use half of that raise to increase your retirement savings contributions and the other half to improve your lifestyle.

The beauty of this simple advice is that you don't miss the money you are contributing to your 401(k) at the start of your career because you have just left school, and you are making more than you ever have before anyway. Also, you don't miss the portion of your raises that are going to increased retirement contributions because the other half of the raise is going towards improving your lifestyle. Life gets better as your finances improve. Ooh, la, la!

There are a few different choices for retirement savings if you do not have access to a 401(k) or 403(b) or similar plan. If you are self-employed or own your own business, you can set up a Solo 401(k) or SEP IRA. Anyone can contribute money to a Traditional or Roth Individual

Retirement Account (IRA). Additionally, a Health Savings Account (HSA) is another way to save money for medical expenses and retirement.

Choosing between a Traditional or Roth IRA is difficult because to make the perfect decision, you have to be able to predict the future. Simply put, if you think your current tax rate is higher than the one you will pay in retirement, choose a Traditional IRA. Otherwise, choose a Roth IRA. If you are unsure, it is almost always best to invest in one or the other type of IRA account rather than neither one.

Do not shortchange saving for retirement to fund a business, an extravagant wedding, or to fund your child's education at an expensive school. One of the greatest gifts you can give your children is not to have to rely on them for money when you are older. If you must decide between retirement savings or saving for your children's education, it is almost always better to save for your retirement. Importantly, saving for your retirement should help to relieve your children of the burden of caring for you in your old age.

Retirement savings should be long-term investments, so it is essential to look at long-term historical returns. According to a 2012 Credit Suisse study of several decades of stock returns, stocks returned an average of 9.3% per year, treasury bonds returned 5.0% per year, and short-term interest returns were less than that. I have seen numerous studies of stocks for many long-term periods and have never seen a study that found stocks returned less than 9% yearly. Keeping in mind that there is no guarantee that future returns will match past performances, these studies point out why stocks seem to be the wisest investment for the long-term.

What about the worst long-term returns' stocks have ever earned? A 2013 Wisdom Tree Asset Management study looked at the history of U.S. stocks since 1871. The study found that the worst 30-year period return was 4.2% per year. Please note that this period included the Great Depression. We certainly all want to earn more than 4.2% per year from our stock investments over 30 years, but I find it comforting to know that even during the period that included the Great Depression, stocks had a decent return. Significantly, a 4.2% return is better than the average return that a short-term interest account earns.

The superior historical long-term returns from stocks are the main reason I heartily recommend that anyone under the age of 40 invest all of their retirement savings in stock mutual funds. The stock mutual fund should preferably be a total stock market index fund with extremely low annual fees. Twenty-five years before your planned retirement date, it is okay to start contributing a portion of your retirement savings to a bond mutual fund. At that time, I would advise limiting your bond investment to 20% of your savings. Once you get to within ten years of your retirement, it is okay to put up to 10% of your retirement funds into short-term interest investments.

The rule of thumb is that you should have at least a percentage of your retirement savings in stocks greater than 120 minus your age. For example, if you are 30 years old, 120 minus 30 equals 90. Therefore, according to this rule of thumb, a 30-year-old should have *at least* 90% of their retirement savings in stocks. According to this rule, a 50-year-old should have at least 70% of their retirement savings in stocks.

I firmly believe the evidence strongly supports the decision to have the vast majority of your retirement savings invested in stocks until you get less than twenty years from retirement. It is best to start investing early for retirement, invest mostly in stocks, and invest in tax-deferred retirement accounts.

If you want to understand long-term investments and retirement planning (and you are willing to put considerable effort into understanding investing, I suggest that you join the

American Association of Individual Investors (AAII), the website is aaii.com. As I write this, a one-year membership costs $49 a year. I am a lifetime member. If I have a complaint about AAII, it is that they provide too much information. My complaint might be "praising with faint damnation." They call themselves a "nonprofit educational publisher." I agree with this assessment.

A straightforward way to reduce risk and increase average investment return is to dollar-cost average. Dollar-cost averaging involves investing the same amount of money every period, usually every month, in the same investment(s). By default, employer retirement plans such as a 401(k) or a 403(b) use dollar-cost averaging. The advantage of dollar-cost averaging is that it will lower the average purchase price of the investment, thus increasing our return.

There is a huge advantage to starting your retirement savings when you are young. If you start young, you can take advantage of the power of compound returns. Compound returns is similar to compound interest. Compound interest is when you not only earn interest on your original deposit, but you also begin to earn interest on interest. Over time, you will start to make more interest on interest than the interest you are earning on your original deposit. With compound returns, you not only earn money on your initial investment but on your earlier returns from the investment. Like compound interest, your profits from your previous gains grow exponentially with time.

I want to emphasize that you should start saving for retirement immediately, even if you are starting at a late age. In this case, better late than never definitely holds. Please, do not use past failures to save as an excuse not to start saving today. After all, have you ever heard anyone complain that they had too much money saved for retirement?

I strongly advise you to avoid annuities even if they are sold to you by what appears to be a knowledgeable and friendly person from an extremely reputable financial firm.

Avoid Investing Mistakes

In investing, luck is often mistaken for skill or knowledge. Many beginning investors make a killing on a few investments early on and become convinced that it is because they are very skillful. They become assured they can keep on picking outstanding investments. Then reality hits. The winners become losers, and they stop investing.

It is essential to note the difference between betting and investing. Bettors, on average, lose money after expenses. Investors, on average, earn money.

Historically, a widely diversified stock portfolio or stock mutual fund has earned an average annual return of around 8% - 10% for the long-term. Some have made some valid arguments why these returns could be marginally lower in the next twenty years. Indeed, these returns can be very negative for periods of less than five years. Still, the hard evidence suggests that stocks are an excellent investment over the long-term.

Often, when one group of people is thriving in an investment for the short-term, other investors pile into similar investments quickly. In this scenario, the price of investments can promptly become divorced from the actual value of the investments. Prices rise rapidly on the hope that someone else will buy the stake from you at an amount higher than you paid for it. This is called a bubble. Bubbles can go on for quite some time, but you do not want to be holding the investment when the bubble bursts and the value of the investment plummets. There will probably be times when you hear that you are a fool if you do not invest in something that is going up in value at an incredible rate. Don't believe it. Don't be the greater fool.

In general, if an investment sounds too good to be true, it almost certainly is a bad idea. It might be a complete scam. For example, let's say I offered you a guaranteed 15% yearly return on your investment, whether the stock market went up or down. That is too good to be accurate and is a scam. In fact, this is very similar to the promise that one of the most successful scammers of all time, Bernie Madoff, made to his investors.

Here are some tips for avoiding scams. First, be very wary of anything that sounds too good to be true. Second, don't invest in anything you do not fully understand. Third, do not trust someone entirely merely because they appear to be respectable. Finally, don't trust someone simply because they are in a group you belong to, whether that group is religious, racial, ethnic, or rests on another similar bond.

Warren Buffett, perhaps the most successful investor of all time, states that rule number one of money is "never lose money." His second rule of investing is "don't forget rule number one." John Bogle, the founder of Vanguard and pioneer of index investing, put it well, "successful investing involves doing a few things right and avoiding serious mistakes." Let's look at some mistakes that should be avoided.

If an investment that sounds too good to be true, it probably is, and you should pass on it. Any investment promising high returns with little or no risk is not to be trusted. In general, stay away from investments that you do not understand.

I advise you to avoid penny stocks (stocks that sell for less than $5 a share). I also advise against buying Over the Counter (OTC) stocks and stocks listed in the pink sheets. Another disadvantage of buying stocks that are not trading on the New York Stock Exchange (NYSE) or the NASDAQ exchange is that the NYSE and NASDAQ have standards of financial stability. They verify that the companies listed on their exchanges are legitimate companies that meet specific criteria. This extra vetting is a valuable benefit to the investor. It is *not* a guarantee that the company will not go bankrupt or commit fraud, but it is an excellent protection against the probability of these occurrences.

Do not short stocks (bet that a stock's price will go down). Do not by stocks or other investments on margin (borrow money to make investments). Do not buy call or put options. Investing in commodities and futures is also not advisable. There are legitimate reasons for some experts to invest using shorts, options, commodities, and futures. There is *no* reason for a non-expert to use them.

Over the long-term, an investment in gold has roughly matched the rate of inflation. But, with storage and insurance costs, gold has an even lower return. Over the long-term, stocks and bonds have handily beaten inflation with no need for insurance or storage costs. I would avoid investing in gold. My only investment in gold is my wife's and my wedding rings. At least, that has proved to be an excellent investment in gold for the long-term.

I advise you to buy collectibles if you enjoy having them and you can afford them. I don't recommend you to view them as suitable investments, even if they may work out that way if you are fortunate or are an expert in the field. Collectibles don't pay interest or dividends to you. Conversely, they usually cost you because of insurance, maintenance, and storage. That is why I advise you to view them as entertainment with a possible investment kicker and not as a significant part of your investment portfolio.

Another problem is that collectibles don't always go up in value. Many can soar for a while, then stagnate, and then eventually decline, sometimes to the point that they have little or no value. Don't be fooled by returns that appear to be extraordinary over the long-term. These returns can be revealed as ordinary or low returns once the annual return is calculated.

Investing in Stocks

You can be a very successful investor without ever investing in individual stocks. Consequently, my advice for most people is to forgo investing in individual stocks. Stock mutual funds are a preferable alternative for most people. Investing in a low-fee diversified stock mutual fund, such as Vanguard's S&P 500 index fund, will give you the superior returns of investing in stocks while significantly reducing your risk and effort.

I always advise investing at least $50,000 in stock mutual funds before investing in individual stocks. Starting your stock investments using mutual funds is simply the best way to achieve a diversified (safer) investment portfolio in stocks without sacrificing high returns.

After making a substantial investment in stock mutual funds, investing in individual stocks can be beneficial. You should never invest more than 10% of your portfolio in any one stock. Research indicates that a diversified portfolio requires at least 25 stocks in it to be considered safe. These stocks should be in different industries to achieve true diversification. For example, investing in 25 oil company stocks offers very little diversification.

The only logical reason to invest in individual stocks instead of a low-cost stock index fund is that you think you can earn higher returns through reduced taxes and fees or superior stock picking. Saving money on taxes and fees is possible through careful planning and discipline. Beating the market through exceptional stock picking is much more challenging.

It is not a good idea to invest money that you think you will need in the next few years in stocks. Stocks are simply too volatile to be an acceptable choice for short-term (less than five years) investments.

Unfortunately, many investors sell in a panic after stocks fall and buy stocks after they have gone up a great deal. This behavior results in "selling low and buying high." That is not a good plan. It is much better to "buy low and sell high." Realistically, it is best to buy quality stocks at a reasonable price and keep the stock for years or forever.

Over the longer term, stocks outperform "safer" investments. Also, although high inflation is not usually beneficial for stocks, stocks do better than most investments during times of high inflation. Historically, a diversified stock portfolio has *never* lost money for a 20-year period. In general, stocks have a significantly higher return over the long-term than bonds, real estate, bank deposits, and other "safer" investments.

Dollar-cost averaging is merely investing the same amount of money every period, with the period usually being monthly or with each paycheck. Most Americans invest in their retirement plans (401k, IRA, 403b) this way. Additionally, many choose to invest in other investments using dollar-cost averaging. That's a good thing because dollar-cost averaging has advantages. If you use dollar-cost averaging, when the price of the stock is down, more shares are purchased.

Similarly, when the price of the stock is up, fewer shares are purchased. Thus, we are buying more shares when the price is low and fewer shares when the price is high. That's a good thing because we are accomplishing the first part of the investors' creed of "buy low and sell high." This is a significant advantage of dollar-cost averaging.

It should be noted that dollar-cost averaging is more effective in purchasing mutual funds that generally move with the market and rarely go to zero than in buying individual stocks. This is because the stock of a single company can go to zero and stay there if the company goes bankrupt. In this scenario, dollar-cost averaging would not save you from losing your entire investment. Still, dollar-cost averaging into reliable mutual funds as most people do in their retirement investments is a powerful and recommended strategy for almost everyone.

When investing in stocks, one of the best ways to do better than the average investor is to avoid common mistakes that many investors make. Failing to diversify investments adequately is a prevalent mistake. Diversification requires investing in a wide array of assets. A typical diversified portfolio would include stocks, real estate, and bonds. It is important to remember that if you own a home or other land for your personal use, that is also an investment.

When investing in stocks or stock mutual funds, diversification is particularly important. The easiest way to diversify stock investments is to invest the majority of your stock-related investments into a widely-diversified stock mutual fund such as an S&P 500 index fund. A simple way to think of diversification is that you are not putting all your eggs in one basket. It is irrational to fail to diversify your investments properly.

Checking on your investments would seem like a wise thing to do, but that is not always true. It is smart to monitor your finances regularly. But it is not a great idea to monitor long-term investments on a daily or weekly basis. Checking investments too frequently can result in anxiety and poor decisions. Monitor your long-term investments, such as retirement plans monthly, quarterly, or yearly. Don't fret overly about fluctuations in value because they will happen. Above all, don't panic and sell when your investments are at a low point.

In general, avoid using beta, technical analysis (charting), and stop-loss orders. If you do not know what these are, you don't need to know.

Over the past 100-plus years, value stocks have had higher returns than growth stocks. Value stocks generally have a lower stock price to earnings per share (P/E) ratio and lower stock price to accounting book value per share (P/B) ratios. Value stocks generally tend to have lower growth rates in sales and earnings. These types of stock are designated as "value" stocks because the investor is thought to be getting a good value by purchasing the stock's sales and earnings at a low or "value" price.

Conversely, growth stocks generally have higher price-earnings (P/E) ratios and higher price to book (P/B) ratios. Also, growth stocks tend to have higher growth rates in sales and earnings, hence the "growth stock" moniker. Depending on the long-term period measured, value stocks have managed to earn about 1% per year more than growth stocks.

Much like the differentiation between value and growth stocks, the stocks of smaller companies have earned higher average returns than the stocks of larger companies over the last 100-plus years. Smaller companies have a smaller market capitalization. Market capitalization (market cap) is the value of all of the company's stock shares (stock price times the number of shares). In general, stocks are broken down into three categories based on the size of the company: small-cap, mid-cap, and large-cap.

Over the past 100-plus years, small-cap stocks have had higher returns than large-cap stocks. In general, small-cap stocks have earned around 2% more per year than large-cap stocks over the long-term. Small-cap stock prices fall much more during market downtrends and rise much more during good times. This volatility can be unnerving to the average investor.

Over a forty- or fifty-year period, a difference in annual return of 1% or 2% is dramatic, perhaps a difference of hundreds of thousands of dollars. It is not uncommon for growth stocks to provide better returns than value stocks for 10-year periods or more. Similarly, large-cap stocks can outperform small-cap stocks for an extended number of years.

One can purchase mutual funds that invest in small-cap, mid-cap, large-cap, value, growth, small-cap value, small-cap growth, large-cap value, and large-cap growth stocks. Also, extended market index funds that invest in all of these types of stocks are available.

The world and economic frameworks are ever-changing. Therefore, the relative returns of value and growth stocks and small-cap and large-cap stocks may be different over the next hundred years.

There is strong evidence that most investors hold onto their losing stock investments too long and sell their winning stock investments too soon. Once I learned of this typical irrational investing behavior, I reviewed my investments and realized that I was guilty of this mistake.

The rationale behind selling winners too soon is, "I have made a lot of money on this investment, now I can sell it and lock in my gain." Yes, you indeed lock in a gain, but that does not mean that you aren't giving up immense future profits. The rationale behind holding on to losers too long is "if I hold on until the investment earns a positive return, I haven't lost money." The problem with this rationale is that the investment may not return to a profitable position *ever*. The investment may languish for years or decades with a negative return, or the value of the investment may even go to zero.

Theoretically, we should not pay any attention to our past returns on an investment. Ignoring past performances is logical because what we paid for an investment in the past is irrelevant. We will not get that money back, no matter what we do in the future. Past investments are called sunk costs, and they should be ignored. The only exception is if we are considering selling a stock for tax management purposes. If we are selling a stock for a gain, we may want to sell another stock for a loss to offset this gain for tax purposes (and vice versa).

Investors that are interested in investing in dividend stocks should pay attention to two dividend measures. A higher dividend yield indicates a higher cash income return on the investment. A lower payout ratio indicates that the company is more likely to continue paying a dividend or even raise the dividend.

An advantage of owning dividend stocks is that the dividends can be soothing to investors during stock market downturns. When the market turns down ten, twenty, or thirty percent or more, it is easier to hang on to your stock investments and not sell in a panic when your dividend payments continue to keep coming. The dividend payments do tend to continue even during bad economic times because the management of most firms work very hard to make sure they can keep paying the dividend even if business is not great.

Congratulations on Your Accomplishment! Now, Keep Going.

Once you learn the basics of personal finance (which you have done if you have read this book or just this chapter), you are not done. Drat! On the other hand, learning the basics of personal finance is an admirable accomplishment that many people do not achieve. Pat yourself on the back. No, really, do it…good.

If you only read this chapter, the first step in your continuing financial education is to read all of this book. That's a short putt. First of all, you have already bought the book. Secondly, the book is exceptionally well-written, and the author is delightfully engaging ☺

Despite your accomplishments, many of the details of personal finance change every year. These details can have a significant impact on your finances. Therefore, you owe it to yourself to keep up on the changes.

Fortunately, information on the current financial environment and tax changes and other economic issues is widely available online and elsewhere. It does take some effort to educate yourself on important financial changes, but it is well worth the work.

There are many reliable sources of advice on personal finances. I have learned more over the years from *Barron's*, *Forbes*, and *The Wall Street Journal* than I learned in my graduate-level finance college classes. This is not meant as an indictment of my graduate college education in finance, but as a complement to what can be learned from these informative financial publications.

If you have a significant investment portfolio of several hundred thousand dollars or more and you have the time and inclination to spend a considerable amount of your time managing these investments, I suggest that you join the American Association of Individual Investors (aaii.com). AAII is also a great organization if you simply want to educate yourself about the particulars of personal finance decisions. Membership in AAII includes a monthly magazine and free website access. They often have conferences with great speakers (for an extra fee) and local meetings available to members.

The cost of membership at AAII is quite reasonable. As I write this, a one-year membership is $49, a 3-year membership is $99, and a lifetime membership is $490. I bought a lifetime membership several years back at about half of the current lifetime membership price. I am delighted that I did so. Of course, the younger you are, the more the lifetime membership makes sense.

I congratulate you on your effort in trying to learn what you can on personal financial management. If you continue to try to learn as much as you can about personal finance, I firmly believe that it will benefit your life and happiness in general.

Money cannot buy happiness, but lack of money can prevent happiness. Money is not the root of all evil, but a lack of money is the root of lots of evil.

I hope that you live long and prosper and that you use your prosperity to make your life and those of your loved ones better. I also hope that you support worthy charities with the wealth that you earned through your hard work and wise decisions. Mahalo.

Appendix A – Print and Post this Checklist

21 Steps to Financial Success

1. You control your financial future. Don't blow it.

2. Save 3 to 6 months' worth of living expenses in emergency savings.

3. Save: ***"If you don't save money, you will always be poor!"***

4. Evaluate education and career choices at least once a year.

5. Decisions regarding marriage, life partners, and children are the most important decisions, financial and otherwise.

6. Friendships should be mutually beneficial.

7. If something doesn't make you money or make you happy, don't do it. Giving to charities and helping others should make you happy.

8. Creating and *using* a budget is *essential* to financial success.

9. Make short-term and long-term financial goals and evaluate your progress regularly.

10. Pay your credit card balances in full every month.

11. Look for opportunities to save money on recurring, monthly, or yearly expenses.

12. Don't buy a home unless you want to live in that home for at least five years.

13. Automobile expenses are a significant expense that you should look to reduce.

14. Start saving for retirement and your children's college as early as possible.

15. Long-term investments should be invested in stock and bond mutual funds.

16. If anyone depends on you financially, you need life insurance and a will.

17. Make sure that you have appropriate health, disability, and automobile insurance.

18. If you have access to a retirement plan with employer matching contributions, contribute as much money as your employer will match. Don't turn down "free money."

19. Every time you get a raise, use half of that raise to increase your retirement savings contributions and the other half to improve your lifestyle.

20. Diversify your investments. Don't put all your eggs in one basket.

21. Continue your personal finance education.

About the Author

Rick Scott spent most of his childhood in poverty, like trailer park and free school lunch poor. He joined the U.S. Army to serve his country and to get money for college. It worked. After graduating from the University of Georgia, Rick was working temp jobs and still living in his mother's double-wide (admittedly one of the more beautiful homes in the park).

Then things started to click. Rick got a corporate job and spent hundreds of hours learning about personal finance. Soon, Rick began to accumulate some wealth. He worked for some of the finest corporations in the world: AT&T, Home Depot, and Publix. Rick also earned a master's in finance from Georgia State University and a Ph.D. in finance from the University of South Florida.

Currently, Dr. Scott is an associate professor at Saint Leo University. He greatly enjoys giving financial advice. Dr. Scott is very happily married to the love of his life and has two beloved teenage daughters. He hasn't been poor for a very long time and wants to keep it that way.